WHY THE BIBLE IS SO HARD TO UNDERSTAND

...and tips to understanding it

STEVE LANGFORD

This book is dedicated to
all who want to understand the Bible
and who want to put its teachings into practice.

ACKNOWLEDGEMENTS

This material was first presented to the members of First United Methodist Church of Georgetown, Texas. Their response to the original study encouraged the writing of this book. I thank God for them, for their response and encouragement, and for their desire to know the Scriptures so they may live as the followers of Jesus.

This book is written in deep appreciation for the many teachers who have taught me the scriptures on my spiritual journey. They laid for me a solid foundation for interpreting the Bible, teaching me *how* to think, not necessarily *what* to think. I thank God for them and their shaping influence on my life.

This book is the product of and a testimony to God's transforming work in my life. The grace of God, as revealed in Jesus the Christ, is the only explanation of who I am today. Any insights I have received and any ability to express those insights to others are gifts of grace from the Spirit.

TABLE OF CONTENTS

INTRODUCTION

The Bible – the sacred scriptures for Christians – is read and studied more than any other book in the Western world. Christians turn to the Bible for guidance and direction in what to believe and how to live. They seek comfort, peace, hope, guidance, and reassurance from its teachings. In this quest to know what the Bible teaches, Christians gather each Sunday in classes to hear it taught and in worship to hear it proclaimed. During the week, groups gather in churches and homes to study it while many individual Christians read it daily.

Yet, for many, the Bible continues to be a difficult book to read and understand. As a result, many do not read the Bible themselves. They depend upon others to tell them what the Bible says and means.

This brief book is an attempt to address the challenges that one encounters in reading the Bible.

* ❖ Chapter 1 – *Why Is the Bible So Hard to Understand?* – deals with the worldview and nature of scripture. How a person views scripture (i.e., his understanding of the nature of scripture) shapes how that one reads and interprets the Bible.
* ❖ Chapter 2 – *How Do I Read the Bible so that It Makes Sense?* – addresses the challenge of

interpretation: understanding what the Bible means. This chapter provides a simple model for interpreting what the Bible says along with helpful hints for using the model.

❖ Chapter 3 – *Isn't There a Simple Way to Understand the Bible? Guiding Principles and Foundational Truths* – provides foundational principles to use in interpreting the Bible.

❖ Chapter 4 – *How Do All the Pieces Fit Together?* - provides an overview of the 2000 years of history reflected in the Bible.

❖ Chapter 5 – *How Do I Know What to Believe?* – addresses the issue of spiritual discernment, summarizing the material as a guide for exercising Spirit-directed discernment.

These chapters offer guidelines for understanding and negotiating the challenges one encounters in reading and understanding the Bible. These guidelines train the reader to interpret scripture so that she is no longer completely dependent upon others for understanding what the Bible means. Yet, even as one grows in his ability to understand scripture, he never outgrows the need for someone to guide them – a teacher.[1]

Questions are included at the end of each chapter for use in personal reflection and journaling. A study guide is included at the end of the book for small group discussion.

CHAPTER ONE

WHY IS THE BIBLE SO HARD TO UNDERSTAND?

When the Spirit of truth comes, he will guide you into all the truth – John 14:13.

S o what makes the Bible so difficult to read and understand, anyway? Simply put, the Bible is not like most books. It is different. Consequently, it cannot be read as one would read a novel or a science book or a book of poetry or a newspaper.

Four factors contribute to the unique nature of the Bible and, thereby, to the difficulty in understanding it.

1. The Bible is actually sixty-six different books rather than a single book.
2. These sixty-six books are ancient books.
3. The sixty-six books are of Near Eastern origin.
4. The sixty-six books are written from a prescientific, theological worldview.

SIXTY-SIX BOOKS

The Bible is not a single book. A glance at the table of contents in any Bible will show that the Bible is comprised of sixty-six different books (in the Protestant Bible). The Catholic Bible includes an additional seventeen books known as the Apocryphal or Deuterocanonical books. These seventeen books are Jewish writings from the period of time between the end of the Old Testament and the beginning of the New Testament.

These sixty-six (or eighty-three) books do not narrate a continuous story from beginning to end, making the story line difficult to follow.[1] Unless the reader understands this fact, it is easy to become confused, get lost, and give up.

These sixty-six books have two separate but closely related foci. The focus of the thirty-nine books of the Old Testament is on the nation of Israel and her relationship with God. These books, along with the Apocryphal/ Deuterocanonical books, contain Israel's history, religious practices, writings, music, and beliefs. The focus of the twenty-seven books of the New Testament is the ministry of Jesus of Nazareth (the four gospels) and the movement that grew out of his ministry (the story of the Church). The ministry of Jesus and the life of the Church are seen as growing out of Israel's history and bringing it to fulfillment, thus continuing the work of God on earth. Understanding these different foci is a part of making sense of the Bible.

These sixty-six books contain many different types of literature: history (more accurately, interpreted history), poetry, songs, epic narratives, prophetic discourses, letters, parables, proverbs, sermons, gospels, and apocalyptic works.[2] Note: nowhere in scripture is there any kind of material that can be described as scientific! The biblical materials were written *before* the development of scientific thought. In learning to interpret the Bible, the reader must understand what kind of literature she is reading and interpret it accordingly.

These sixty-six books are the works of over forty different authors, compilers, and editors. The books of Genesis through Deuteronomy (the Pentateuch) reflect the work of an editor who used at least four different identifiable sources to develop the work. The book of Psalms is a compilation from numerous sources, organized into five different books.[3] The book of Isaiah reflects the work of three different authors from three different periods of time: Isaiah 1-39, 40-55, 56-66. The book of Lamentations is a compilation of five different poems lamenting and interpreting the destruction of Jerusalem in 586 B.C.E. Some of the authors are identified in the works themselves.[4] Other works are anonymous, including the four gospels (Matthew, Mark, Luke, and John), the book of Acts, Hebrews, and 1, 2, & 3 John. Some authors followed the common practice of writing in the name of another, highly respected individual from an earlier time – e.g., Daniel, 1 & 2 Timothy, Titus, 1 & 2 Peter. Understanding who wrote what book, at what time, in what setting is a vital key to understanding the Bible. Such information is readily available in any quality study Bible.

ANCIENT BOOKS

The material in these sixty-six books is old. The earliest material – Genesis 2-11 – consists of epic narratives that were passed down from generation to generation by word of mouth, long before being recorded. The stories related to Abraham (Genesis 12-25) date to 1750 B.C.E. while the Exodus story dates around 1250 B.C.E.

The Babylonian invasion of Judah, resulting in the first deportation of Jewish citizens to Babylon, began in 597 B.C.E. The destruction of Jerusalem and final deportation took place in 586 B.C.E. The return from exile began in 538 B.C.E. with an edict from the Persian king Cyrus. The rebuilt temple was dedicated in 515 B.C.E.

The thirty-nine books of the Hebrew scriptures were collected and compiled during and following the Babylonian exile experience (586 – 515 B.C.E.). The destruction of the nation, Jerusalem, and the Temple in 586 B.C.E. robbed the nation of its primary sources of identity. To reestablish that identity within a refugee situation in a foreign land, the scholars began the process of collecting and compiling their history and their writings. The two histories – Deuteronomistic history[5] and the history of the Chronicles – were written during the Exile. 200 years before the birth of Jesus, the Hebrew Scriptures had been compiled and translated into Greek. These books were the scriptures that Jesus and the Apostle Paul studied and used.

The Apostle Paul's letters were the earliest New Testament material to be written. His earliest letter, the book of 1 Thessalonians, dates to 50 C.E. All of the letters of Paul were written before the destruction of the Temple in Jerusalem by the Romans in 70 C.E. The Gospel of Mark was probably written just before the Jewish revolt that led to Jerusalem's destruction in 70 C.E. The other three gospels were written after that cataclysmic event. The last books of the New Testament to be written date to about 100 C.E.

From beginning to end, the material in the Bible covers almost 2000 years of history. That means that the material in the Bible is from 3750 years to 1900 years old. Understanding the historical period in which and

16

to which a particular text was written is a part of understanding the Bible.

NEAR EASTERN BOOKS

All sixty-six books of the Bible are products of the ancient Near East. The books reflect multiple ancient Near Eastern cultures: Hebrew, Egyptian, Philistine, Assyrian, Babylonian, Persian, Greek along with two Ancient Western cultures: Roman and Corinthian. Each culture had a different language, customs, worldview, gods and religious practices. Understanding the characteristics of these ancient, Near Eastern cultures puts the reader in a position to understand the biblical material.

Each of these ancient cultures was tied to an agricultural economic foundation: flocks of sheep and goats and camels, wheat and barley, grapes and vineyards and figs.

In the beginning of Israel's history (Abraham & the patriarchs, Genesis 12-50), the people were nomads, moving within a geographical area according to the needs of their herds. As Israel moved into the land of Canaan after the Exodus, they moved from being a nomadic people to being an agricultural people settled on the land. As they settled Canaan (Joshua, Judges), each tribe and each family within the tribe were allotted plots of land as their own. During that time, they shifted from a nomadic lifestyle to a settled one. This new lifestyle involved farming, requiring them to learn a new way of life. This shift helps to explain the inclination of the Israelites to follow "other gods" – specifically, the Canaanite fertility gods. The people were seeking to guarantee the fertility of their crops and flocks by following the practices of the Canaanite farmers who were there before them.

The period of the Hebrew Kingdom (1 & 2 Samuel, 1 & 2 Kings) reflects the development of cities and trade. The walled cities became the center of commerce as well as the means of security. In times of danger, the people would go inside the city where the city gates would be closed and barred for protection. The city gates became places of legal transactions.

The later cultures were composed of two classes of people: (1) the upper class who were privileged, wealthy, and powerful, and (2) the laboring class who were poor, powerless, and exploited by the wealthy. This exploitation underlies many of the prophetic messages proclaimed by the Hebrew prophets.[6] Slavery was common in most of these cultures, particularly in the Roman Empire.

This two-class system was a hierarchal system. When Israel settled the land of Canaan, the people attempted to be egalitarian. Every family was allotted land – a place of their own. They functioned without a centralized government – no king or governor. This egalitarian approach to life was an intentional rejection of the hierarchal system they had experienced in Egypt, a system they had experienced from the bottom of the hierarchy as slaves! As the people began to desire the security offered by a king, the prophet Samuel resisted their desires, warning them of the dangers of the hierarchal system associated with a king (1 Samuel 8:4-22). With the beginning of the monarchy, the egalitarian culture began to pass away as did the loss of the family allotments. The story of Naboth's vineyard (1 Kings 21:1-16) is an example of how the wealthy began to take possession of the land, creating an impoverished class of working poor. The prophet Amos condemned such exploitation of the poor.[7] Isaiah 5:7-8 condemns this practice of building large estates at the expense of the poor.

Most of these ancient cultures were patriarchal cultures.[8] A man was the head of every family and every system. Consequently, every woman was under the authority, protection, and provision of a man, either her father or her husband or her adult son. In patriarchal cultures, a widow or an orphan had no man to protect or provide for them. Thus, the Hebrew Scriptures emphasize God's concern for the widow, orphan, alien, and poor – those who were powerless, without social protection and provision.[9]

The books of the Bible were originally written in Near Eastern languages: Hebrew, Aramaic, Greek. Every English Bible is a translation from these original languages, a process that involves interpretation.

PRESCIENTIFIC, THEOLOGICAL UNDERSTANDING OF THE WORLD

Each of these ancient, Near Eastern cultures lived out of a pre-scientific, theologically defined worldview. Religious and spiritual terms were used to explain that which the people did not understand. Life's events were commonly attributed to the work of the gods and various spirits. For example, King Saul suffered from some kind of paranoia, depression or mental illness, but it was explained as an evil spirit (1 Samuel 16:14-16, 23). A boy's seizures - possibly epilepsy - were explained as an evil spirit seizing him (Mark 9:17-18, 20-27). One understanding among the ancient Hebrew people was that illness, calamity, and poverty were punishment from God (see John 9:1-3) whereas God rewarded righteousness with health, long life, wealth, and a large family. The dialogue in the book of Job revolves around this

19

kind of thinking. Job's friends argue this perspective as an explanation for Job's suffering while Job maintained his innocence and, thereby, the injustice of his suffering. Several books in Hebrew scripture reflect the influence of this kind of thinking, including Job, selected Psalms, Proverbs, and Ecclesiastes. This kind of thinking is found in what Biblical scholars refer to as Wisdom literature.

The ancient Hebrews' understanding of creation was a theologically shaped understanding. They viewed creation as a three-story universe: the heavens as the realm of God (or the gods), the earth as the realm of humans, under the earth as the realm of the dead. This three-tiered universe is behind the story of the Tower of Babel (Genesis 11:1-9) in which humans attempted to invade the realm of the gods by building a tower to heaven. This understanding is reflected in the account of Jesus' ascension in which he was taken up in the clouds (Acts 1:9-11). To be taken up into the clouds was to move into the realm where God dwelt. This understanding is behind the practice of speaking of heaven as "up".

The ancient people believed in a multitude of gods. Thus, the cultures of the ancient Near East were full of gods. Every nation had a god and, sometimes, multiple gods - a god for each different aspect of life. As every nation had its own god or gods, the gods were viewed as territorial. The power and authority of the nation's god were thought to extend only over the territory of that nation. The god's power and authority ended at the country's border. Thus, when nations went to war, the war was viewed as a war between the gods of the warring nations. The god of the victorious nation was viewed as the more powerful god.

This understanding of territorial gods is the backdrop to the Exodus story. The Exodus story is portrayed as a conflict between Israel's God Yahweh (the LORD) and the gods of the Egyptian pantheon. In Exodus 5:2, the Pharaoh asked: *who is the LORD* (Yahweh), *that I should heed him and let Israel go? I do not know the LORD, and I will not let Israel go.* The ten plagues are portrayed as Yahweh's response to the Pharaoh's question. Each plague attacked a different god in the Egyptian pantheon, demonstrating that Yahweh was the true God over each aspect of Hebrew life. This view is expressed in Exodus 12:12 – *on all the gods of Egypt I will execute judgements: I am the LORD.* A recurring theme throughout the narrative of the ten plagues is God's self-revelation to the Egyptian people: *that you may know that I am the LORD* (6:7; 7:5, 17; 8:10, 22; 9:14, 29; 10:2, 14:4). The story relates a growing recognition of Yahweh among the priests of Egypt, among the people, and even from the Pharaoh himself.[10] The story of the ten plagues ends with the gods of Egypt defeated and the people of Egypt plundered, language associated with victory in battle (Exodus 12:33-36).

The Hebrew people, before the Exile, lived out of this understanding of multiple gods. The prophet Hosea condemned the people of the northern kingdom of Israel for being unfaithful, forsaking the worship of Yahweh and worshipping other gods. The Hebrew people viewed God as a Divine Warrior, the Lord of Hosts (armies). The king sought God's guidance in battle (1 Samuel 13:5-15; 14:36-37). In Psalm 44:9-11, the psalmist lamented that God did not go out with them to fight, thus allowing them to be defeated. The understanding of territorial gods at war also explains the practice of slaughtering people and animals following a victory.[11] The slaughter was viewed as a sacrifice to the victorious god – to the victor goes the spoils!

This thinking in terms of multiple gods and the behavior associated with it ended with the Exile experience. The unnamed prophet of the Exile (Isaiah 40-55) gave voice to a new understanding: the LORD (Yahweh) was the creator of the heavens and earth and, thereby, the Lord of history.[12] The LORD was at work in history to accomplish divine purposes on behalf of God's people.[13] Israel was not in Exile because the LORD was defeated but because the LORD gave the people into bondage as punishment for their sin.[14] All other so-called gods were mere idols, man-made images with no power.[15] Following the experience of the Exile, there is no record of the people of Israel ever worshiping other gods as they did before the Exile.

These four factors all contribute to the difficulty that one encounters in attempting to read the Bible. The Bible is sixty-six ancient, Near Eastern works that were written from a pre-scientific, theologically-interpreted worldview.

The Bible is 66 ancient, Near Eastern works that were written from a pre-scientific, theologically-interpreted worldview.

In addition to these four factors about the Bible itself, two other factors contribute to the difficulty one has in reading and understanding the Bible. These two factors are tied to the reader: the worldview of the reader and the already-held beliefs of the reader.

THE WORLDVIEW OF THE READER

Whereas the Bible is an ancient, Near Eastern work written from a pre-scientific, theologically shaped worldview, the worldview of today's readers of the Bible is just the opposite. Those who read the Bible today are trained to think from a worldview shaped by the Enlightenment, Western thought, and the scientific process.

The Enlightenment refers to a European revolution in thinking associated with the late 17th and 18th centuries. Although this revolution in thinking took place over 300 years ago, it continues to influence thinking in the 21st century – including how today's readers read the Bible. Enlightenment thinking is associated with the rejection of tradition, the questioning of authority, the emphasis upon individualism, the ideas of freedom and equality, the reliance upon human reason, the development of scientific thought, and the confidence in human progress. Such thinking led to the development of democracy, capitalism, and public education. It also led to the development of a belief called deism. Deism espouses the belief that God created the universe but is not directly involved in its functioning. Rather, creation operates through the natural laws that God set in place. Humans were given reason to use in understanding this ordered creation. Deism rejects any supernatural dimension of religion, including the idea of revelation or miracles or the divinity of Jesus. Human reason replaced divine revelation as the measure for truth.

The continued evolution of Enlightenment thinking has produced what is called post-modern thought. Post-modern thinking rejects any external standard of right and wrong. Objective truth is replaced by subjective relativism. What works for a particular individual is what is "right" for that person. Post-modern thought is expressed in the saying, "It's all good."

Enlightenment shaped thinking is inseparably tied to scientific thought. Scientific thought uses human reason to understand creation. The scientific method, which asks "who, what, when, where, why, and how," lies at the heart of public education. Explanation of that which is not understood is sought through scientific inquiry, experimentation, and theory. Scientific understanding, based upon human reason, is viewed as the way to progress.

Current Western thinking is shaped by these three factors: Enlightenment thinking (sometimes called modernity) or post-modern thinking, Western thinking, and scientific thought. They are the milieu that shapes how the Western reader unconsciously thinks. Thus, anyone from the Western world today who seeks to read the Bible does so out of a modern or post-modern, Western, scientific worldview. The Western reader brings that thinking to an ancient, Near Eastern book (or books) that are written from a pre-scientific, theological worldview

The Bible's Nature	*The Reader's Nature*
Ancient	*Modern & Post-modern*
Near Eastern	*Western*
Pre-scientific, theological worldview	*Scientific worldview*

For example, Western scientific thought equates truth with fact. A Western reader would identify the statement "this book is printed on white paper" as a true statement. Trained to think of truth as fact, the reader of the Bible today reads looking for facts to believe. The Bible is read as though it were a book filled with historical and scientific facts.

The ancient, Near Eastern writers were not interested in facts as much as they were interested in truth. For the ancient, Near Eastern writers, the statement "this book is printed on white paper" would be viewed as an accurate statement, not necessarily a true statement. For them, truth was more than – and greater than – accurate facts. Thus, they wrote to communicate what they understood about God and life and human beings – what they would call truth.

The ancient, Near Eastern writers communicated truth by telling a story or reciting poetry. Their story communicated truth that was more than and greater than scientific facts. Facts – what, when, where, why, how – were merely vehicles for communicating truth. One feature of ancient Hebrew writing was to use facts that were not "accurate" in telling a story to communicate what they knew to be true. The truth was more important than the facts.

The failure to understand the ancient, Near Eastern, pre-scientific worldview from which the Bible was written leads to Western, scientifically-oriented questions which the Bible was not written to answer - nor does it answer! Did God create the world in seven literal days? Were Adam and Eve the first two human beings? Did Moses really part the Red Sea? Did Jesus really heal people or walk on water? Was Jesus physically raised from the dead? These kinds of questions are Western, scientifically-oriented questions that are focused on facts. Such scientifically-based questions are being asked of ancient, Near Eastern, theologically-oriented books. The thinking and language of science is being used to interpret poetry and story.

Asking such Western, scientifically-oriented questions of the Bible is a barrier to understanding the Bible. Such questions lead to speculation and needless controversy. When the Bible does not specifically answer the question being asked, the reader frequently speculates in an effort to answer his own question. Or, the reader misuses the Bible to make it say something it was not intended to say. The greatest tragedy, however, is that the reader, by asking the wrong questions, misses what the passage really *is* saying. When the Bible does not answer a question the reader is asking, then the reader is being invited to ask a different question: what was the biblical writer attempting to communicate to the original audience?

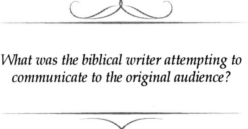

What was the biblical writer attempting to communicate to the original audience?

If one is to understand the Bible, it must be read as an ancient, Near Eastern work – particularly a Jewish work - not as a product of Western thought.

THE ALREADY-HELD BELIEFS OF THE READER

A second, reader-related factor that complicates the effort to understand what the Bible says is what the reader already believes. Each reader comes to scripture with a belief structure – a theology. Those beliefs are ones the reader has been taught or picked up somewhere along the journey. Every reader, without exception, reads scripture through the lens of those beliefs.

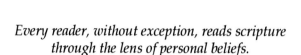

*Every reader, without exception, reads scripture
through the lens of personal beliefs.*

Reading through the lens of one's own beliefs is normal and unavoidable. The danger comes when the reader is not conscious of this belief-shaped lens. When the reader does not recognize this set of inherent lens, he unconsciously reads with a bias, looking for confirmation of what he already believes. Thus, he expects what is already believed, looks for what is already believed, and sees what is already believed. This bias-of-belief blocks the reader's ability to recognize what the text is actually saying. More, this bias fosters resistance to what the scripture actually says when it is different from what one already believes. As a result, the reader uses the Bible to reinforce how he already thinks rather than allowing the truth of scripture to shape his thinking.

In the story of The Garden (Genesis 2-3), for example, a serpent enticed the man and the woman to disobey God's one directive: don't eat of the tree of the knowledge of good and evil (Genesis 2:16-17; 3:1-5). An untrained reader is quick to identify the serpent as Satan or the Devil. Yet, nowhere in the text is there a reference to Satan. In fact, the word "Satan" is only used in 3 places in Hebrew scripture: Job 1:6-12; 2:1-7; Zechariah 3:1. In each of these places, the word is not a proper name *Satan* but a noun with an article: the accuser, the adversary. Understanding the serpent in Genesis 3 as a reference to Satan is reading a New Testament understanding of Satan back into the Hebrew story.

Another expression of this belief-bias is one's familiarity with a biblical passage. What the reader already thinks the passage says can blind him to what the passage actually says. For example, a common understanding of John 14:1-3 is that Jesus was going to prepare a place in heaven for the believer and, then, he would return. Yet, the world "heaven" is not used anywhere in John 14 or in the larger context of John 13–16. The place Jesus prepared for his followers was a place in relationship with the Father. Jesus was the one through whom the disciples had come to know God as Father (14:6, 9). In going away, Jesus was not abandoning them or leaving them as orphans (14:18). The Spirit would come to be for them another Companion like Jesus had been (14:16), who would dwell in and among Jesus' followers (14:17). In the Spirit, Jesus and the Father would come make their home in the life of the disciple (14:23, the word *home* in verse 23 is the exact same word in the original that Jesus used in verse 2 in reference to the place he was going to prepare). Jesus' teaching was about the intimate, indwelling relationship his disciples would have with God through the Spirit. Familiarity hinders one's ability to grasp what the original author intended for his original audience.

So what makes the Bible so difficult to read and understand, anyway? A combination of these factors creates the difficulty:

- ❖ the ancient, Near Eastern, pre-scientific worldview of the sixty-six books that make up the Bible;

❖ the Enlightenment-shaped, scientifically oriented worldview of the modern Western reader; and
❖ the belief-shaped lens through which the reader reads the Bible.

FOR PERSONAL REFLECTION:

1. When did you first begin to read and study the Bible? How has your reading and study of the Bible changed over the years?
2. This book and this chapter in particular assume that many readers find the Bible difficult to understand. What kind of struggles have you experienced in reading and trying to understand the Bible? How have those struggles affected you and your reading of the Bible? Identify an example of something in the Bible that you do not understand.
2. This chapter describes the Bible as sixty-six ancient books that were written from a Near Eastern, prescientific, theological world view. How does this description help you to understand your struggle in understanding the Bible? How might this understanding of the Bible guide how you read it?
3. This chapter indicated that reading out of scientifically trained thinking can be both a barrier and an advantage to understanding the Bible. Identify an example of both in your own experience.
4. Relate an example of a belief you surrendered through studying the Bible.
5. What in this chapter was helpful to you? Why? What in this chapter stirred discomfort or angst in you?

Chapter Two

HOW DO I READ THE BIBLE SO THAT IT MAKES SENSE?

You will know the truth, and the truth will make you free –
John 8:32.

In spite of the challenges one faces in reading and understanding the Bible, these challenges can, with training and practice, be overcome. Interestingly, one of the challenges to reading and understanding the Bible – the Enlightenment-shaped, scientifically-oriented worldview of Western thought – can be a valuable resource in learning to interpret the Bible.

The key to interpreting scripture is to let it be what it is: an ancient, Near Eastern, pre-scientific, theologically-oriented work – specifically, a Jewish work. The discerning reader will learn to use his reason-based, scientifically trained thinking to read the Bible as an ancient, Near Eastern work. That kind of scientifically trained thinking can help the reader identify the ancient, Near Eastern, pre-scientific dimensions of the text, thereby leading to greater understanding of the text.

THE TASK OF INTERPRETATION

Interpreting what the Bible says and means cannot be avoided. Every person who reads the Bible is also involved in interpreting it. Some may say, "I just believe what the Bible says" or "I take what the Bible says literally."[1] Without realizing it, that person chooses a method of interpreting the Bible. Unfortunately, it is a method of interpreting the Bible that frequently leads to misinterpretation.

Every person who reads the Bible interprets it.

A literal reading of the Bible is not actually possible. Every reader brings to the task his own set of beliefs and understandings (as addressed in the previous chapter). When one seeks to read literally, that one unconsciously reads through the lens of his own theological worldview and belief system. Consequently, attempting to read the Bible literally is an almost certain guarantee of reading one's beliefs *into* what the Bible says. Literal interpretation almost always leads to misinterpretation.

The only choice that the reader of scripture really has is what kind and quality of interpreter will he be.

Interpretation is the task of discerning what the author was trying to say to his original audience. That task involves identifying two parts of a text: (1) the truth the biblical writer wanted to communicate and (2) the manner in which that truth was communicated. *What* the author wanted to communicate to his audience was a gem of truth about God. *How* the author delivered that gem was in an ancient, Near Eastern, pre-scientific, theologically-oriented wrapping. Interpretation is the task of removing the wrapping to get to the gem. The more the reader understands *how* the writer communicated, the more the reader can understand *what* the writer was communicating.

Another way of speaking of these two dimensions of a text is to speak of the human dimension of scripture and the divine dimension of scripture. These two dimensions of scripture can be seen in 2 Peter 1:19-21 - *First of all you must understand this, that no prophecy of scripture is a matter of one's own interpretation, because no prophecy ever came by human will, but men and women moved by the Holy Spirit spoke from God.*

*The Bible has both a human dimension and
a divine dimension.*

The human dimension of scripture is expressed in the phrase *men and women moved by the Holy Spirit spoke from God.* Men and women spoke at a particular time, in a particular place, in a particular setting, to a particular people in a particular situation. The writer of the book of Hebrews expressed this human dimension this way: *Long ago God spoke to our ancestors in many and various ways by the prophets* (1:1). This statement expresses …

when God spoke – *long ago;*
to whom God spoke – *our ancestors;*
how God spoke – *in many and various ways;*
through whom God spoke – *by the prophets.*

This human dimension of scripture is the ancient, Near Eastern, pre-scientific wrapping in which the gem was delivered. The more the interpreter can identify the different aspects of the wrapper, the easier it is to recognize the gem.

The gem is the divine dimension of scripture. It is the timeless, eternal truth that is applicable to anyone in any given culture or time. The text from 2 Peter says that those who spoke did not just proclaim their own thinking about God or speak out of their own will. Rather, they were moved by the Holy Spirit. The Hebrews 1 text emphasizes that God spoke. God spoke through human beings as prophets, but it was God who was speaking through them. 2 Timothy 3:16 states *all scripture is inspired by God.* The word inspired carries the imagery of God-breathed. Just as God breathed the breath of life into the man and he became a living being (Genesis 2:7), so God breathed life into the scriptures.

Throughout Hebrew history, culminating in Jesus of Nazareth, God was seeking to reveal the Divine Self to human beings. The Bible is the record of that self-revelation. The Bible is not the record of human speculation about God but rather the record of God's divine self-communication. It is not the record of human groping after God but rather the record of God's seeking to be known. In God's self-revelation and self-communication, God was reaching out to establish relationship with humankind whom God created.

The Hebrew Scriptures or Old Testament are the record of God's self-revelation to the people of Israel throughout their history – up to the Roman era. The Christian scriptures or New Testament is the record of how the people called Christians understood God's self-revelation in and through Jesus of Nazareth.

Because of this divine dimension of scripture, the scriptures hold great value for those who would know God and live as the followers of Jesus. The writer of 2 Peter urged his readers to pay attention to scripture *as to a light shining in a dark place* (1:19). The writer of 2 Timothy said the scriptures were *useful for teaching, for reproof , for correction, and for training in righteousness, so that everyone who belongs to God may be proficient, equipped for every good work* (3:16-17). The writer's statement about teaching and reproof is in reference to what to believe. The statement about correction and training is in reference to how to live one's beliefs. Thus, the divine dimension of scripture guides the reader in what to believe and how to live.

God spoke through the prophets. The Spirit moved men and women to speak for God. The scripture is God-breathed. Each of these statements points to the divine dimension of scripture. The implication of this divine dimension is that God was behind the writing, collecting, and publishing of the scriptures. It suggests that God still uses the scriptures to speak today. Through the study of scripture, readers today can know what God has revealed of the Divine Self and what God has communicated of God's eternal purpose in the world. The interpreter, under the guidance of the Holy Spirit, can know …

(1) the character of God
(2) the ways of God
(3) the eternal, divine purpose of God.

Understanding these two dimensions of scripture – the human, the divine - is foundational for understanding the Bible.

Understanding these two dimensions of scripture – the human, the divine - is foundational to understanding the Bible. Some readers focus on one of the two dimensions, ignoring or denying the second. This one-dimensional focus skews how one reads scripture and, consequently, what one believes.

Some focus only on the divine dimension. These readers read everything written in the Bible as coming straight from God, ignoring the human dimension of scripture. They use such words as infallible and inerrant to describe the Bible. Such reading can lead to misinterpretation or misapplication of scripture as cultural mores of another time and place are viewed as binding today.

Others focus only on the human dimension, denying the divine dimension. These readers view the Bible as merely a human product. They seek to understand the *who, what, when, where, why,* and *how* dimensions of scripture while rejecting any part of scripture that relates anything supernatural (miracles, the incarnation, the virgin birth, or the resurrection). This way of reading the Bible is the product of Enlightenment thinking that exalts human reason as the means to human progress and rejects any kind of divine intervention in human affairs.

Recognizing both the human dimension and the divine dimension of scripture guides the reader in identifying the truth of God communicated within a human wrapper. Understanding the human dimension of scripture helps the reader understand the nature of God's self-communication.

THE NATURE OF GOD'S SELF-REVELATION

Hebrews 1:1-3 helps us to understand God's self-revelation as recorded in scripture. *Long ago God spoke to our ancestors in many and various ways by the prophets, but in these last days he has spoken to us by a Son, whom he appointed heir of all things, through whom he also created the worlds. He is the reflection of God's glory and the exact imprint of God's very being, and he sustains all things by his powerful word.*

This text presents a four-fold contrast in how God has spoken:

in the past	in these last days (the days of the first disciples)
to our forefathers	to us (the author and his readers)
through the prophets	by his Son
at many times and in various ways	(unexpressed; implied is fully, completely, finally)

This four-fold contrast suggests three facts regarding God's self-revelation:

(1) it was partial rather than complete;
(2) it was accommodated;
(3) it was progressive.

The Hebrews 1 text states that God spoke in the past *at many times and in various ways*. The original language carries the idea of "in bits and pieces". God's self-revelation before Jesus was always *partial*. The prophets who spoke *to our forefathers* had only glimpses of God, not a full view.[2] The contrast drawn in the verses suggests that the most complete revelation of God was *by his Son*. The Son is described as *the reflection of God's glory and the exact imprint of God's very being*. Thus, God's fullest and most complete self-revelation was in Jesus of Nazareth.[3]

God's partial self-revelation was due to the people's inability to grasp more. God started where the people were. Thus, in addition to being partial, God's self-revelation was *accommodated*. God only revealed as much as the people at that time could comprehend. In accommodating to the ability of the people to understand, God expressed the Divine self-revelation in the historical-cultural setting of the day. For example, in the Decalogue given at Mt. Sinai, God commanded the people *you shall have no other gods before* (or besides) *me* (Exodus 20:3). This commandment reflects the ancient belief in many gods. The command was for Israel to have an exclusive relationship with Yahweh rather than Yahweh being just one among many gods that they worshipped. As was presented in Chapter 1, the belief in God as the only God (monotheism) developed much later during the Exile.

Many readers today are offended by what they read in the Hebrew Scriptures. These offensive pieces, such as the slaughter of enemies in the name of God, were a normal part of the culture of that ancient time. When a modern reader is offended by practices recorded in the Hebrew Scriptures, the reader is overlooking the partial, accommodated nature of God's self-revelation. The reader is projecting New Testament or current beliefs and practices back onto people who did not have the advantage of God's fullest self-revelation in Jesus of Nazareth.

Throughout the history of Israel, God was guiding the people into a fuller understanding of God's nature and God's ways. Thus, the Hebrew Scriptures reflect a growing understanding of God's self-revelation, with the fullest understanding coming in and through Jesus of Nazareth. An example of this *progression* of understanding is seen in the issue of retaliation. In Genesis 4:23-24, Lamech, the great-great-great grandson of Cain, swore unlimited retaliation on any who wronged him: *I have killed a man for wounding me, a young man for striking me. If Cain is avenged sevenfold, truly Lamech seventy-seven fold.* The Book of the Covenant associated with Mt. Sinai prescribed limited retaliation to offset unlimited retaliation: an eye for an eye, a tooth for a tooth (Exodus 21:22-25). Jesus spoke of non-retaliation (Matthew 5:28-42) and unlimited forgiveness, using the expression originally used by Lamech to speak of unlimited forgiveness – seventy-seven fold (Matthew 18:21-22). Unlimited retaliation gave way to limited retaliation which gave way to non-retaliation and unlimited forgiveness.

In the midst of this progression of understanding, selected individuals experienced leaps in understanding, moving far beyond the contemporary understanding. Moses received a revelation of God's character (Exodus 34:6-7) and of the unconditional nature of God's covenant relationship with Israel.[4] In spite of this revelation, the nation continued to relate to God out of a conditional framework. Yet, Moses' understanding of the character of God continued to surface in Israel's thought as seen in Psalm 103:7-14 and Jonah 4:1-2. The prophet Jeremiah, 600 years before the birth of Jesus, proclaimed a new covenant that was rooted in God's forgiveness in place of the conditional *if ... then* covenant of Exodus 19 (Jeremiah 31:31-34). This covenant would result in God's laws being written on the hearts of the people (internal transformation) rather than on tablets of stone. An unnamed prophet in the Exile moved beyond the common belief that suffering was God's punishment for sin to understanding that suffering could be redemptive (Isaiah 53).

Understanding the partial, accommodated, progressive nature of God's self-revelation guides the reader in understanding scripture. It reminds the reader that not all scriptures are equally useful in knowing God and the ways of God. Some passages express more of the human dimension of scripture (the historical, cultural context) than revealing the divine dimension (the eternal truth about God and the ways of God). Thus, the reader is to look for those texts that reveal the character of God and the ways of God, particularly those passages that reflect a leap in understanding of God and the ways of God. Understanding the partial, accommodated, progressive nature of God's self-revelation also reminds the reader that everything identified as *truth* will align with the teachings and practices of Jesus, God's fullest self-revelation. The life and teachings of Jesus are foundational for understanding the ways of God.

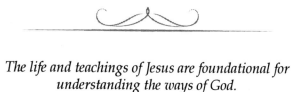

The life and teachings of Jesus are foundational for understanding the ways of God.

A MODEL FOR INTERPRETING SCRIPTURE

Understanding the nature of God's self-revelation as recorded in the Bible helps the reader understand the goal or objective of interpretation. That goal is to (1) identify, (2) understand, and (3) apply the divine truth communicated by the biblical writer within a specific historical, cultural context. In other words, the objective in interpreting the Bible is to unwrap the gem of truth about God from its ancient, Near Eastern, pre-scientific, theologically-oriented, human wrapping. Learning to read the Bible is like eating pieces of hard candy that are individually wrapped. In order to get to the candy, one must remove it from its wrapper. The wrapper is discarded and the candy consumed. Failure to distinguish between the wrapper (the human dimension) and the candy (the divine dimension) can leave the reader chewing on a wrapper rather than enjoying the sweetness of God's truth. Getting to the divine truth requires identifying the wrapper that contains it.

This unwrapping process is reflected in the model:[5]

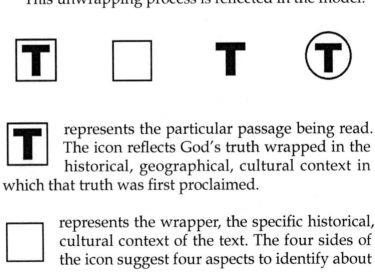

T represents the particular passage being read. The icon reflects God's truth wrapped in the historical, geographical, cultural context in which that truth was first proclaimed.

represents the wrapper, the specific historical, cultural context of the text. The four sides of the icon suggest four aspects to identify about the text: (1) the historical context - *when*, (2) the geographical and cultural context – *where* and *who*, (3) the type of literature, key words, and expressions of language - *how*, (4) the larger context surrounding the specific text. Most passages contain hints as to the historical, geographical, cultural context as well as to its type of literature and language.

T represents the divine truth – the unwrapped gem. The divine truth is that which is timeless and eternal and, thereby, applicable to anyone in any given culture or time.

Ⓣ represents God's truth applied to one's own life in the specifics of one's own historical, culture situation. The objective of reading the Bible is not information, but transformation – a life shaped by God through the teachings of Jesus as recorded in scripture. This icon represents how the divine truth is lived out in the particular context of one's own life.

GUIDELINES FOR USING THE MODEL

(1) Read the text.

Read the text carefully and slowly, paying attention to the progression of the story or thought process. Identify what happened in the passage and what was said. Identify terms, individuals, places, customs, answering Who? What? When? Where? How? Why? Some find it helpful to read the text in several different translations or in a translation that is new to the reader.

Key question: What happened? What was said?

41

(2) Identify the scriptural context.

Each passage is to be interpreted within and in light of its context. Every verse is a part of a paragraph which is a part of a section which is a part of a chapter which is part of a book which is part of the Old or New Testament which is part of the Bible. The context - that which goes with the text - is a guide to the thought or meaning of the passage. The author's flow of thought in the larger section guides how one understands a particular passage.

Key question: How does the text relate to what comes before it and after it?

(3) Identify the historical and geographical contexts.

The author spoke to a specific people in a specific situation that took place in a specific location at a specific time. Understanding what the author said to the original audience becomes clearer as the reader understands the historical and geographical settings..
The books of the Hebrew prophets spoke a word from God addressing a particular situation at a particular time in a particular nation. Understanding that particular situation in a particular time and place guides the reader in understanding the prophet's message. The prophets were not, as commonly thought in popular culture, predicting the future for a future generation. Isaiah 40-55, sometimes referred to as Deutero-Isaiah, was addressed to the people of Judah during their experience of exile in Babylon. The prophet's poems addressed the people's feeling of abandonment, guiding them to think of God in a new and different way. The book of Revelation is a prophetic book, using

apocalyptic imagery, spoken to the churches of Asia Minor during a time of great persecution. The author wrote a message of assurance and hope that called for patient endurance and faithfulness in the face of persecution.

Sometimes the historical context of the people being addressed is not the same as the story being presented. In these situations, the reader must identify the historical context of both the story and the intended audience. Three such books are Ruth, Jonah, and Daniel. The setting of the story of Ruth is the period of the judges, before the monarchy was established. The backdrop of Jonah was Israel's conflict with the Assyrians before the nation fell in 722 B.C.E. These two stories, set in different historical contexts, address issues that surfaced in the nation of Judah after their return from exile (after 515 B.C.E.). The writers of these two works spoke to the people seeking to resettle the land after the Exile. They did so by telling stories set earlier in Israel's history. This same technique was used in writing the book of Daniel. The historical setting for the story of Daniel was the Babylonian captivity. The story was told as a way of communicating hope to people living in the post-exilic period.

Key questions:
When and where did this happen?
For whom was it written?

(4) Identify cultural issues.

The original audience was shaped by the culture in which they lived. Each text reflects aspects of the culture, beliefs, practices, and traditions of that original audience. Identifying those aspects in the text helps the reader to understand the situation being addressed. For example, the book of Revelation was addressed to Christians being persecuted in Asia Minor for their failure to express allegiance to Caesar. Such allegiance was expressed in worshipping at a statue of Caesar and proclaiming "Caesar is Lord!" The worship of Caesar is a key cultural piece for understanding the message of this apocalyptic writing.

<u>Key questions</u>:
What in the text is strange to me or difficult for me to understand?
Why was that particular fact mentioned?

(5) Identify the type of literature.

Each type of literature calls the reader to approach and interpret it differently. The law codes found in the book of Exodus are to be read differently than the poetry of the Psalms. The epic sagas of Genesis 2-11 are to be read differently than the story of the church recorded in Acts. The wisdom sayings found in the book of Proverbs are to be read differently than the parables of Jesus. Paul's letters are to be read differently than the prophetic discourses recorded in the prophetic books. The gospels are to be read differently than the interpreted history of 1 & 2 Samuel, 1 & 2 Kings or 1 & 2 Chronicles or the apocalyptic book of Revelation.

<u>Key question</u>: What kind of literature am I reading?

(6) Note the language and grammar.

Pay attention to key words. Identify figures of speech. Watch for parallelism in Hebrew poetry: line A expresses the main thought; line B expresses the same thought in different words or by contrast. Be aware of patterns. The Genesis 1 creation story, for example, repeats the same phrases on each of the six days: God said; and it was so; God saw; it was good; evening and morning. On the sixth day, the phrase "it was very good" replaced "it was good." That shift suggests an important point: the creation of man and woman in the Divine Image was the culmination of creation.

Key question: What words or expressions or phrases seem to stand out as important?

(7) Identify the human condition being expressed in the situation or addressed by the text.

The human condition is that which is common to all people: emotion, need, fears, struggle, and life experience. Every gem of truth contained in the scriptures addresses some dimension of the human condition.

Key questions:
What in the situation is common to all people?
What human condition, point of struggle, emotion or need is addressed in the text?
How have I experienced what these people experienced?

(8) Identify the spiritual truth that addresses that human condition.

The spiritual truth is that which is timeless. It speaks of God, the character of God, and the ways of God. It speaks of human beings and how they normally think, feel, and function. It speaks of the relationship between God and humans.

Key questions:

What is the main idea of the passage?

What did the passage say to the original audience and their situation? What truth is the author attempting to communicate?

What does this passage say about people, about God, about the relationship between people and God, about the relationship between people and people?

What was being said to that people in that situation that continues to be true and applicable today?

(9) Identify how to live out that truth today.

The task of interpretation is not complete until the eternal truth is integrated into the reader's life. The ultimate objective of reading the Bible is transformation, not information. The follower of Jesus allows the truth of God to shape how he thinks and, thereby, lives as opposed to using the Bible to support what he already believes.

Key questions:

What must I do in order to live in harmony with this truth?

How does the eternal truth apply to me and to my relationships?

What does the eternal truth call me to do?

RESOURCES FOR IDENTIFYING THE WRAPPER

While the task of interpreting scripture may appear daunting, today's reader has a multitude of resources to help with the task. The most accessible resource is a good study Bible.[6] Bible dictionaries provide information about culture, geography, history, etc. An atlas contains maps of the biblical regions according to historical periods. Books are available that provide background information and trace the flow of biblical history. Lexicons are a more technical piece that provides meanings of Biblical words. Concordances help the reader see how a particular word is used throughout scripture and the text in which it appears. Most readers are familiar with commentaries and frequently turn to them. The best commentaries are those that help the reader understand cultural aspects essential to understanding the text, the historical situation, and key features of the author's language.

FOR PERSONAL REFLECTION:

1. The chapter identified two different dimensions of scripture: the human dimension and the divine dimension. Identify an example of the human dimension of scripture.
2. Identify an example of how the human wrapper might be confused with the divine truth.
3. Practice using the interpretation model on a favorite passage of scripture.

Identify the human dimensions within the passage – the wrapper in which the divine truth was placed.

What of the human dimension did you not understand or was strange to you – ancient, Near Eastern, prescientific? How does that aspect impact your understanding of the text?

What was the situation being addressed in the text?

What did the author say to the original audience?

What is the divine truth that the text communicates?

4. What in this chapter was helpful to you? Why? What in this chapter stirred discomfort or angst in you? What in this chapter did you not understand?

CHAPTER THREE

ISN'T THERE A SIMPLE WAY TO UNDERSTAND THE BIBLE? GUIDING PRINCIPLES AND FOUNDATIONAL TRUTHS

How can I understand unless someone guides me? –
the Ethiopian eunuch, Acts 8:31

C hapter Two presented a model for interpreting scripture and some practical tips to use with the model. This chapter presents some guiding principles and foundational truths to use in the task of interpretation. These principles and foundational truths will help the reader move beyond the belief-bias identified in Chapter One.

GUIDING PRINCIPLES

Principle #1 – recognize and honor the dual nature of scripture: a human work and a divine work. This principle was developed in Chapter Two. In order to identify the divine truth of a text, identify the human wrapping which carries it.

Principle #2 – follow Jesus' pattern of using scripture.

Jesus did not give equal value and importance to every verse. He was selective in his use of scripture. Jesus commonly used scriptures that reflected the nature of God and the ways of God – what Jesus called the Kingdom of God. Use the scriptures to know God and God's ways.

Jesus did not use the Hebrew Scriptures as a rule book prescribing what to do or not do. Although the religious culture of Jesus' day placed strong emphasis upon the Law and obeying the Law, Jesus refused to get trapped in controversy regarding laws and religious rules. He also refused to abide by many of the religious laws of his day, particularly regarding the Sabbath and that which was unclean. When pressed about the Law, he emphasized the Shema (Deuteronomy 6:5): *you shall love the Lord your God with all your heart, and with all your soul, and with all your mind, and with all your strength,* (Mark 12:33), coupling it with Leviticus 19:18, *you shall love your neighbor as yourself.* For Jesus, the essence of the spiritual life was relational, not behavioral or legal. In the Sermon on the Mount (Matthew 5:17-48), Jesus pressed beyond the letter of the law to the underlying principle. Search the scriptures for guiding principles rather than rules and laws.

Jesus' pattern calls the reader to be discerning in how scripture is used.

Principle #3 – trust and rely upon the Spirit of God to guide your thinking.

In the Farewell Discourses of John's gospel (John 13-16), Jesus taught that the Spirit would both teach his disciples and remind them of what Jesus had taught them (John 14:26). The Spirit would guide them into all truth (John 16:12-15). In his letter to the Corinthians, Paul spoke of the Spirit's role in teaching the deep things of God (1 Corinthians 2:6-16). Just as the Spirit was involved in the writing and collecting of the scriptures (2 Timothy 3:16-17; 2 Peter 1:19-21), so the Spirit guides the reader in the task of interpreting scripture today. Ask the Spirit to guide and teach.

Principle #4 – allow tradition, reason, and experience to guide your understanding. Tradition refers to how a text has been understood throughout Christian history. Reason refers to rational, logical thinking. Reason asks, "Is this understanding reflected throughout scripture? Is it in harmony with the character of God? Does it align with the ways Jesus lived and taught?" Experience involves the personal dimension. How does one's personal experience guide the understanding of the text?

Principle #5 - when in doubt, use the life, teachings, and ministry of Jesus as the standard for discernment.

The standard against which every interpretation is to be measured is the life and teachings of Jesus. Following what Jesus taught and doing what Jesus did will always lead one to God's truth.

The standard against which every interpretation is to be measured is the life and teachings of Jesus.

FOUNDATIONAL TRUTHS

One of the disconcerting facts about the Bible is that it does not present a single theological perspective. Rather, numerous differing positions are found in its pages. The book of Deuteronomy and the history written from its theological perspective[1] present a conditional covenant for living in the land of Canaan. In contrast, the prophet Jeremiah proclaimed an unconditional covenant with individuals based upon God's forgiveness (Jeremiah 31:31-34). Wisdom literature views life from an orderly, structured perspective, teaching that the secret to long life, happiness, wealth, and health was proper living. The book of Job refutes that thinking. The book of Ezra records an ethnic cleansing during the post-Exilic community in which Ezra demanded that the men put away foreign wives and the children born to them (Ezra 10:9-44). The books of Ruth and Jonah were written to counteract such thinking. Wisdom literature teaches that sickness and suffering are the result of sin whereas the unidentified prophet of the Exile proclaimed suffering to be redemptive (Isaiah 53).

Given such differing and sometimes conflicting views, how is one to know which view to embrace as truth? The way through such a maze is to focus on who

God is revealed to be, the ways of God, the divine purpose of God, and the Kingdom of God.

<u>The Character of God</u>

The foundational truth to use in interpreting scripture is the character of God. All spiritual truth grows out of and aligns with who God is. The character of God is the bedrock upon which the foundation is built. It is the sun around which belief and practice revolve. It is the guiding star in understanding spiritual truth. It is the plumb line used to measure all interpretations. All truth grows out of and aligns with the nature and character of God.

All truth grows out of and aligns with the nature and character of God.

The LORD revealed the Divine Character to Moses on Mt. Sinai. The context of that self-revelation included ...

- the LORD's invitation to the people at Mt. Sinai to live in a conditional, *if...then* covenant relationship (Exodus 19:1-8);
- the establishment of the covenant (Exodus 24:1-8);
- the story of the golden calf (Exodus 32). In constructing the golden calf, the people violated the covenant, nullifying it.

- ▪ Moses' intercession with the LORD on behalf of the people (Exodus 33). In this intercession, the LORD led Moses into a deeper understanding of who God is. In response to Moses' request - *show me you glory, I pray* (33:18), the Lord agreed to reveal his goodness to Moses and to proclaim the meaning of the Divine Name, the LORD (Exodus 33:19). That revelation is recorded in Exodus 34:6-7.[2]

Exodus 34:6-7 uses two adjectives to describe the LORD: *a God merciful and gracious*. The two Hebrew adjectives speak of a God who feels for God's people the way a mother feels for her hurting child and who responds with compassion to address their need. Three phrases then clarify what it means for God to be merciful and gracious.

- ❖ *Slow to anger* – God is not easily moved to anger by disobedience and wrong. Rather, God patiently suffers the affront without reacting angrily.
- ❖ *Abounding in faithful love* – the Hebrew word conveys two thoughts: faithfulness and love. This word is regularly used in Hebrew scripture to speak of God's covenant love. The word means that God never gives up on or abandons the one God loves. The abundance of such faithful love is mentioned twice. God abounds in such love; God keeps such covenant love to the thousandth generation.
- ❖ *Forgiving iniquity and transgressions and sins.* These three common Hebrew words for sin suggest that God forgives any and every sin.

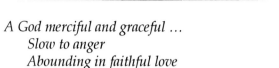

A God merciful and graceful ...
Slow to anger
Abounding in faithful love
Forgiving iniquity, transgressions and sins

This passage speaks of how God deals with sin and failure: by being slow to react with anger, by not giving up on or abandoning the people, and by forgiving the wrong-doing. This response to human failure is just the opposite of how Moses responded to the people in the Golden Calf incident. Moses reacted angrily, breaking the tablets of the covenant (Exodus 32:19) and declaring the covenant broken. He dealt with the people from a posture of us-them (32:25-26) and punished the people for their sin (32:27-28). This revelation of the character of God teaches that God does not deal with sin as humans commonly do.[3]

This passage revealing the character of God ends with a phrase that can be disturbing until it is understood: *yet by no means clearing the guilty, but visiting the iniquity of the parents upon the children and the children's children, to the third and the fourth generations* (34:7c). This phrase proclaims that actions (sins) have consequences. The way God responds to human sin – slow to anger, not giving up on or abandoning, forgiving – does not remove the consequences of human choice. Those choices have wide-ranging impact that reaches to one's grandchildren and beyond - to the third and fourth generation.[4] By contrast, the faithful love of God reaches to the thousandth generation. That contrast proclaims a great truth: even though human sin has painful consequences that touch others, God's faithful love is greater than the sin or its consequences.[5]

Actions have consequences.

Jesus dealt with human sin and failure in keeping with this description of God's character. Jesus responded with compassion and forgiveness. His way of dealing with human failure guided the New Testament writers to see God's nature in Jesus. Thus, they identified him as the fullest revelation of God's character: *the reflection of God's glory and the exact imprint of God's very being* (Hebrews 1:3). *In him, all the fullness of God was pleased to dwell* (Colossians 1:19). *He is the image of the invisible God* (Colossians 1:15). He has made God known (John 1:18).

The biblical writer of 1 John used a single word to describe the character of God: love. *God is love* (1 John 4:8). The Greek word the writer used to describe the essence of God is known as agape love. The following verses (4:9-10) portray agape love as self-giving, other-centered, and seeking the good of the one loved. Jesus embodied such self-giving love.

Servant is another Biblical term used to express the self-giving nature of God's kind of love. Jesus spoke of his ministry as that of a servant: *For the son of man came not to be served, but to serve and give his life a ransom for many,* (Mark 10:35-45). Jesus lived as a servant, using his power on behalf of others, for their good, at great cost to self. In his letter to the Philippians, Paul quoted an ancient hymn that described Jesus as a servant: *who, though he was in the form of God, did not regard equality with God as something to be exploited, but emptied himself, taking the form of a slave, being born in human likeness. And being found in human form, he humbled himself and became obedient to the point of death – even death on a cross. Therefore God also highly exalted him and gave him the name that is above every name, so that at the name of Jesus every knee should bend, in heaven and on earth and under the earth, and every tongue should confess that Jesus Christ is Lord, to the glory of God the Father* (Philippians 2:5-11).

The character of God is one of mercy, grace, and forgiveness. It is one of self-giving, servant love. Any interpretation of scripture that contradicts the merciful and gracious character of God or goes against the self-giving, servant love of Jesus does not accurately present divine truth. The character of God is the plumb line against which all interpretations are measured.

The Eternal Purpose of God

A second foundational truth to use in interpreting scripture is the eternal purpose of God that is revealed in the biblical story.

Most readers come to scripture with an assumption about what this purpose is. This assumption defines God's purpose in terms of salvation for humans. In this understanding, God's purpose was to provide a means, through Jesus, for people's sins to be forgiven, providing them a way to go to heaven and escaping condemnation to hell. This understanding produces a man-centered version of Christianity with heaven as its goal. This popular understanding of God's purpose shapes the way most people read the Bible, blinding them to the larger purpose of God revealed in both the Hebrew Scriptures and the New Testament.

The eternal *purpose* of God revealed in scripture is larger than helping people escape hell and get to heaven. God's eternal, divine purpose is to restore unity and wholeness to all of creation, to both heaven and earth. God is seeking to overcome the alienation that is reflected in creation and marks all relationships. The Genesis 3 story of the Garden reflects four dimensions of broken relationships: individuals with God, with one another, with self, and with creation. The book of Ephesians and the book of Revelation both suggest another dimension of alienation: between God and certain angelic beings (Ephesians 3:9-10; Revelation 12:7-9). God's eternal purpose is to bring reconciliation, restoring oneness and wholeness. God's purpose is to overcome the alienation between God and individuals, between individuals and nations, and within each individual person. Through such reconciliation on earth, God seeks to bring reconciliation between God and the angelic beings in the heavenly realms (Ephesians 3:9-10). Such reconciliation will consequently overcome the brokenness in creation, restoring creation to wholeness. (See Romans 8:18-25; Revelation 21 & 22.) This restored creation will reflect the character of God and follow the self-giving, servant love of God. Jesus spoke of this God-shaped world as the Kingdom of God. The writers of Isaiah (65:17-25) and of Revelation (chapters 21-22) spoke of this restored creation as a new heaven and earth.

God's *strategy* for achieving this divine purpose was to create God-shaped people - a family of sons and daughters who possess the Divine Nature and reflect the Divine likeness. By living the ways of God, this family is God's partner in God's eternal enterprise of creating a God-shaped world marked by reconciliation. This family of sons and daughters consists of the people of Israel, initially, and then was expanded to include the followers of Jesus from every tribe and nation (Romans 9-11; Ephesians 2).

To be God's children is to live in intentional relationship with God as the people of God and the followers of Jesus. This relationship produces a transformation of heart, mind, and life. By living in relationship with God, these children of God and followers of Jesus learn the grace-based, servant ways of God. The Spirit uses that learning to transform how one thinks and, then, how one lives. Like all children, God's children grow. Spiritual growth leads towards the kind of spiritual-emotional-relational maturity that is seen in Jesus of Nazareth. Such growth produces God-shaped people who partner with God in creating a God-shaped world.

This divine strategy, designed to accomplish God's divine purpose, is grounded in God's character of self-giving, servant love. God's character inevitably leads to an all-out effort to bridge any kind of rebellion and alienation – in heaven or earth – by restoring unity through reconciliation. This faithful love knows no limits. God gives the Divine Self to live in relationship with humans – first in Abram, then in his descendants, the people of Israel, and ultimately with all people through Jesus. The incarnation – God taking on human flesh in Jesus of Nazareth (John 1:1-18) – is the logical expression of God's character of self-giving, servant love. The faithful, servant love of God is also expressed in the gift of the Spirit through whom God continues to dwell with and work through God's children and Jesus' followers. The Spirit teaches God's children the ways of God, guides them in how to live God's ways, and empowers them to live the ways of God. Through the Son and the Spirit, God is creating God-shaped people who are God's partners in creating a God-shaped world.

Through the Son and the Spirit, God is creating God-shaped people who are God's partners in creating a God-shaped world.

The biblical story reflects this eternal, divine purpose in a multitude of ways. It is a recurring theme in the midst of the diverse theologies and diverse life circumstances reflected in scripture.

- In the covenant with Abram, God spoke of blessing Abram so that all the families of the earth would be blessed through him (Genesis 12:3).
- In the Sinai covenant with the people of Israel at Mt. Sinai, God spoke of the people as being a priestly kingdom and a holy nation (Exodus 19:6). As God's people, the people of Israel would be priests through whom the rest of the world would know God and God's ways. As a holy nation, they would teach and live the ways of God. Through them, other people would come to relationship with God, embracing the ways of God as their own.
- Both the prophet Isaiah and the prophet Micah spoke of a time when all the nations of the world would come to the people of Judah in Jerusalem to learn the ways of God. This instruction in the ways of God would involve dialogue and negotiations in dealing with disputes, leading to the end of war as a way of international politics. Technology and power previously invested in war would be invested in productivity that

would bless all. *They shall beat their swords into plowshares, and their spears into pruning hooks; nation shall not lift up sword against nation, neither shall they learn war anymore,* (Isaiah 2:4; Micah 4:3).

- The prophet Isaiah envisioned a time of endless peace that would extend throughout creation (Isaiah 9:2-7, 10:33-11:9). Such peace would be the work of God, accomplished through God's anointed messiah as king. The messiah would embody and guide the nation in living God's ways of justice and righteousness. Power would be used to serve and empower rather than to dominant and destroy.

- The prophet Jeremiah foresaw the day of a new covenant (Jeremiah 31:31-34), a radically different covenant from the conditional covenant of Mt. Sinai (Exodus 19:6-7). This new covenant would be based on God's forgiveness rather than human obedience. It would involve personal transformation as God's laws (nature) were written internally on the human heart. This transformation of heart would replace the deeply engrained perverseness of the human heart (Jeremiah 17:1, 9).

- The unnamed prophet to the people of Israel in Babylonian exile spoke of the Servant of the Lord as establishing justice in the earth, as teaching the world the ways of God, and as being a light to the nations. In and through this servant, the LORD was at work to do new things (Isaiah 42:4, 6, 9). Of this Servant, the LORD said: *I will give you as a light to the nations, that my salvation may reach to the end of the earth* (Isaiah 49:6). The work of the Servant would involve suffering (Isaiah 50:4-6; 52:13-53:12). None-the-less, through the suffering of the Servant, God's divine will would prosper (Isaiah 53:10).

- The unidentified prophet to the people of Israel after the Exile envisioned the LORD as creating a new heavens and a new earth – a new creation in which power is no longer used to dominate and destroy. This new creation would be marked by universal peace – extending even to creation (Isaiah 65:17-25).

- The central theme of Jesus' preaching was the Kingdom of God or the Kingdom of Heaven (Matthew 4:17; Mark 1:14-15; Luke 4:43). He taught his disciples to pray *your kingdom come ... on earth as it is in heaven* (Matthew 6:10). He taught and lived the ways of the Kingdom. He used his power to heal and bring wholeness. He embraced all unconditionally, viewing and treating each person as a beloved child of God. He rejected religious laws and practices that violated the ways of the Kingdom.

- The salvation proclaimed by the Apostle Paul focused upon being transformed into the likeness of Jesus. In his letter to the churches in Rome, he wrote: *and we boast in our hope of sharing the glory of God* (Romans 5:2). *For those whom he foreknew he also predestined to be conformed to the image of his Son* (Romans 8:29). *Do not be conformed to this world, but be transformed by the renewing of your minds* (Romans 12:2). This understanding of salvation as transformation permeates Paul's writings. *All of us ... are being transformed into the same image from one degree of glory to another* (2 Corinthians 3:18). *If anyone is in Christ, there is a new creation; everything old has passed away; see, everything has become new! All this is from God ...*

for our sake (God) *made him to be sin who knew no sin, so that in him we might become the righteousness of God* (2 Corinthians 5:17-18a, 21).[6]

- The writer of Ephesians and the writer of Colossians both spoke of a new self that is created in the likeness of God. Using the metaphor of undressing and dressing, both writers exhorted their readers to put off the old self with its self-serving ways and put on the new self. *You were taught to put away your former way of life, your old self, corrupt and deluded by its lusts, and to be renewed in the spirit of your minds, and to clothe yourselves with the new self, created according to the likeness of God in true righteousness and holiness* (Ephesians 4:22-24). *Seeing that you have stripped off the old self with its practices and have clothed yourself with the new self, which is being renewed in knowledge according to the image of its creator* (Colossians 3:9-10; see also Colossians 3:12-17).

- The writer of Ephesians spoke of God's eternal purpose as the mystery of God's will: *he has made known to us the mystery of his will, according to his good pleasure that he set forth in Christ, as a plan for the fullness of time, to gather up all things in him, things in heaven and things on earth.* God's purpose is to restore unity and wholeness to all of creation – heaven and earth. The Apostle Paul spoke of creation as longing for this time (Romans 8:19-25). The writer of Ephesians spoke more of the mystery of God's will in 3:1-13. This mystery had not been known until it was revealed to the apostles in Christ Jesus (vs. 5). The mystery is stated clearly in verse 9-10: *and to make everyone see what is the plan of the mystery hidden for ages in God who created all things; so that through the church the wisdom of God in its rich variety might now be made known to the rulers and authorities in the heavenly places.* God is using the Church, composed of both Jews and Gentiles (2:11-22; 3:6), to demonstrate to those in the spiritual realm the wisdom and beauty of God's ways of self-giving, servant love. God's objective is to restore unity and wholeness to all of creation and to all within creation.[7]

- The book of Revelation ends with a vision of a new heaven and a new earth. This vision of a new creation included a new Jerusalem and a new Garden. In this new creation, the old is gone. The new creation is patterned after the character of God and is shaped by the ways of God. God lives among God's people in perfect fellowship.

God is creating God-shaped people who partner with God in creating a God-shaped world. This God-shaped world operates according to God's ways of justice and righteousness, ultimately resulting in a peace that permeates all of creation. God is working to heal the brokenness that grips both humankind and creation, restoring wholeness through reconciliation. The result will be a new creation – a new heaven and earth, a new Jerusalem, a new Garden (Revelation 21-22) – in which God and humans dwell together in endless shalom. Understanding this larger, eternal, divine purpose of God helps the reader escape belief-bias to recognize a Christianity that is God-centered rather than man-centered.

The Kingdom of God

A third foundational truth to use in interpreting scripture is an understanding of the Kingdom of God that Jesus proclaimed and inaugurated.

Jesus envisioned a world in which the ways of God would be the ways of the world. By reflecting on the way Jesus lived and what he taught, the reader of scripture can identify characteristics of the Kingdom that Jesus envisioned. The God-shaped world that Jesus envisioned is one in which . . .

- people relate to one another the way God relates to us: out of grace and forgiveness. This grace-based way of relating stands in contrast to the conditional, merit-reward, *if . . . then* way of relating that is a normal part of the human condition. Living in healthy, meaningful relationships requires that we deal with human weakness and failure with forgiveness.
- each person – without exception - is embraced, accepted, and valued as a beloved child of God. Each is unique and valued, having gifts to offer the whole. Such unconditional acceptance stands in contrast to the *us-them, better than-less than* thinking that is a normal part of the human condition.
- power is used to serve. In this grace-based, servant use of power, the follower of Jesus walks alongside the other, using one's resources and power on behalf of the other, seeking the other's good and wellbeing, even at great cost to self. The Hebrew prophets referred to this servant use of power as justice. This servant use of power stands in contrast to the self-seeking,

what's-in-it-for-me, power-over spirit that is a normal part of the human condition.

- people are valued more than material things. Relationships are central in the Kingdom. People and relationships take priority. Consequently, material things are used to meet the needs of people, not to be accumulated in an attempt to provide personal security or used as a symbol of status or standing. Again, this valuing of people more than material things stands in contrast to the buy-consume-and-accumulate-more spirit that is a normal part of the human condition. The buy-consume-and-accumulate-more spirit inevitably produces scarcity thinking: there is never enough.

- God-shaped community is central. Each person uses their gifts and abilities in an area of passion in relation to one another so that the community works together for greater good. That which is normal to the human condition is to use one's abilities for financial gain, for the good of self and family.

The values and ways of the Kingdom are to be the ways of the followers of Jesus. Each church is to be an expression of the Kingdom of God in its community. Each congregation is to offer the world in which it resides an alternative way of thinking, relating, and living. The more a congregation embodies the ways of the Kingdom, the more they will be out-of-step with the culture in which they live.

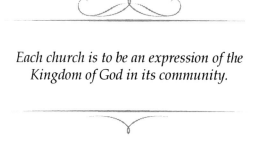

*Each church is to be an expression of the
Kingdom of God in its community.*

Grace

A fourth foundational truth to use in interpreting scripture is an understanding of the grace of God.

God relates out of God's merciful and gracious character – out of God's self-giving, servant love – rather than in reaction to what a person does. The New Testament term used to express how God relates is *grace*. Grace means that God unconditionally accepts, freely forgives, and joyfully embraces each person as a beloved child. God faithfully walks in relationship with each one, teaching the servant ways of love and guiding each person's growth in those ways. Grace communicates that God forgives each sin, using the failure as an opportunity for growth. The word *grace* includes God's promise to bring this divine work of transformation to completion, bringing each person to Christ-like spiritual maturity.

Grace-based relating stands in stark contrast to the way humans normally relate. The default pattern of human relationships is based upon earning and deserving. This earning-deserving, merit-reward pattern is expressed in *if...then* relating. "If you ..., then I will ...." "If you believe like me and look like me, I will accept you. If you hurt me, I will reject you. If you apologize, I will forgive." In this *if...then* way of relating, what one person is or does determines what the other does. This pattern of relating is conditional.

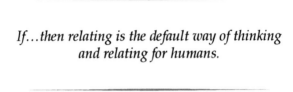

If...then relating is the default way of thinking and relating for humans.

Grace-based relating is unconditional. This kind of relating grows out of who God. It is not dependent upon who the other is or what the other does. God's grace-based way of living and relating is foreign to normal human thinking. Thus, grace-based living must be learned and consciously embraced. Learning to think and live out of grace is part of the renewing of the mind of which the Apostle Paul spoke (Romans 12:2).

Because *if...then* relating is the default way of relating for humans, humans unconsciously seek to relate to God in this way. The result is a merit-reward, earning-deserving based religious life. Grace-based relating produces a radically different kind of spiritual and religious life than does *if...then* thinking and relating.

❖ In grace-based relating, God is the <u>initiator</u>. The individual responds to what God has done. That response is called faith (thus, the theological term grace and faith).In *if...then* relating, the individual is the initiator. The individual acts in an attempt to gain a response from God. God's response is based upon what the individual does or does not do, i.e., merit. God's response is a reward that is earned by obedience and conformity to expectations and demands.

❖ In grace-based relating, the <u>emphasis</u> is upon the relationship with God and growing in that relationship. In *if...then* relating, the emphasis is upon the expectations to which one must measure up. *If...then* relating involves rules and laws, a code of beliefs, behavior (ethics), and ritual to which one must conform in order to gain a response from God or others.

❖ Grace-based relating <u>focuses</u> upon the interior realm of the heart. This internal realm is the realm of thoughts and feelings, attitudes and spirit. God works to transform the heart. *If... then* relating focuses upon the external – one's behavior and actions. The individual works to control his behavior and actions.

❖ The <u>goal</u> of grace-based relating is transformation and spiritual growth. The goal of *if...then* relating is conformity of belief, behavior, and religious ritual in an attempt to gain acceptance.

❖ Grace-based relating <u>produces</u> authenticity and genuineness. It leads to radical self-honesty and to openness with others. *If...then* relating leads to an over-focus on appearances. It produces superficiality and pretense in relationships and to spiritual blindness within one's self.

❖ The <u>tone</u> of grace-based relating is unconditional. God's acceptance and forgiveness are gifts freely and lavishly given. The tone of *if...then* relating is conditional. Acceptance is based upon conformity of belief, behavior, and religious ritual. Forgiveness must be gained through confession and repentance. Failure to live up to expectations results in one "getting what you deserve."

Frequently, the one who metes out these "just deserve" is the individual himself.

❖ Grace-based relating is <u>rooted in</u> one's walk with God, guided and empowered by the Spirit. The relationship with God is marked by glad dependency upon God's faithful love. In contrast, *if...then* relating is rooted in self-effort. The relationship with God and what one receives in that relationship depend upon one's self-effort.

❖ Grace-based relating leads to a <u>spirit</u> of love and thanksgiving in relation to God. It is expressed in praise, adoration, and gratitude. *If...then* relating plays on a spirit marked by guilt and fear, judgment and condemnation.

❖ The <u>reward</u> in grace-based relating is participation in God's quality of life – now and after death. The term *eternal life* is used in the gospel of John for this God-kind of life. The reward offered in *if...then* relating is heaven – life after death. The punishment for failure is hell.

❖ In grace-based relating, <u>power</u> is used in the religious community to serve and empower, to bless and nurture. Power is used out of Jesus' servant spirit. In *if...then* relating, power is used in the religious community to produce conformity. Failure to measure up is condemned and punished. Power is used the way it is used in the world - over the other, controlling and dominating for the benefit of the one who holds the power.

❖ Grace-based relating produces a <u>church</u> that is an inclusive, nurturing community. All are valued and embraced as beloved children of God. Relationships express the radical hospitality of the grace of God. The community makes disciples of Jesus by nurturing spiritual growth. *If...then* relating produces a religious group that is exclusive. The community thinks out of an *us-them* mentality. Acceptance and belonging are for those "like us" in belief, behavior, and religious ritual.

❖ Churches that operate out of grace-based thinking generally use <u>scripture</u> as a tool to know God and the ways of God. The recorded experience of others becomes a guide to one's own experience of living in relationship with God. These churches speak of scripture as the record of God's self-revelation. Exclusive religious communities relating out of *if...then* thinking tend to view scripture as an absolute authority for determining proper belief, behavior, and religious ritual. These communities speak of scripture as the authoritative, infallible, inerrant word of God.

❖ Churches that operate out of grace-based thinking become an expression of <u>the Kingdom of God</u> on earth. Exclusive religious communities relating out of *if...then* thinking become another religious expression of normal human thinking and relating.

The reader who desires to understand the eternal truth recorded in scripture will read with an awareness of grace as God's pattern of relating. The understanding of grace will help the reader escape the *if...then* belief-bias that is inherent to human thinking and relating.

FOR PERSONAL REFLECTION:

1. One of the guiding principles offered in this chapter was *follow Jesus' pattern of using scripture*. What guidelines can you draw from Jesus' use of scripture?

2. This chapter asserted that the Bible does not present a single theological perspective. Identify an example of differing theological perspectives in scripture. What is the implication of this reality for interpreting scripture?

3. The first foundational truth that was presented was the character of God. How does your understanding of the character of God compare with the description of the character of God presented in this chapter? What role does the character of God play in interpreting scripture?

4. *God's strategy for achieving this divine purpose was to create God-shaped people - a family of sons and daughters who possess the Divine Nature and reflect the Divine likeness. By living the ways of God, this family is God's partner in God's eternal enterprise of creating a God-shaped world marked by reconciliation.* How does this description compare to your understanding of what it means to be a Christian?

5. This chapter used the terms *man-centered Christianity* and *God-centered Christianity*. What is the difference between these two expressions of Christianity?

6. The Kingdom of God was a third foundational truth identified in the chapter. What place has the Kingdom of God had in your spiritual journey?

What is the relationship between the Kingdom of God and the Church?

Review the 5 characteristics of the Kingdom of God presented in the chapter. Which one seems to be most challenging?

Identify an expression of the Kingdom of God in your church life.

6. The fourth foundational truth identified in this chapter was God's grace-based way of relating. When and how did you first began to understand God's grace?

What kind of struggle does grace create for you?

Identify an example in your experience of each kind of relating: grace-based, merit-reward.

Where do you see grace-based relating in your church life? Identify an example of merit-reward based relating in church life.

7. What in this chapter was helpful to you? Why? What in this chapter stirred discomfort or angst in you? What in this chapter did you not understand?

CHAPTER FOUR

HOW DO ALL THE PIECES FIT TOGETHER?

*Long ago God spoke to our ancestors in many
and various ways* – Hebrews 1:1.

How do all of the sixty-six books of the Bible fit together? How does the reader make sense of 2000 years of biblical history? How does the reader follow the story line over that length of time?

A tool that addresses such questions is an outline of the different historical periods found in scripture. Such an outline is like the straightedge of a jigsaw puzzle. Once the straightedge pieces are put together, they form a framework within which to work. The consecutive periods of Hebrew history provide a similar framework within which the reader can work. Eight different periods of history can be identified in the Bible:[1]

The Period of the Beginnings
The Period of the Hebrew Patriarchs and Matriarchs
The Period of Egyptian Slavery and Deliverance
The Period of the Conquest and Settlement of Canaan

The Period of the Hebrew Monarchy
The Period of the Babylonian Exile and Restoration
The Period between the Testaments
The New Testament Period.

THE PERIOD OF THE BEGINNINGS:
Genesis 1-11

The first historical period in scripture is the Period of the Beginnings. This period is found in the first eleven chapters of Genesis. This section of scripture includes an intricately designed creation poem (Genesis 1) and four epic narratives that were originally passed down by word of mouth from generation to generation. These five units are tied together by a series of genealogical tables. The focus of these epic narratives is humankind in general. Each story communicates theological truth rather than describing actual historical events.

This period sets the backdrop to the creation of the nation of Israel.

THE PERIOD OF THE HEBREW PATRIARCHS AND MATRIARCHS:
Genesis 12-50

The story of the nation of Israel begins with the story of their forefathers and foremothers: Abraham and Sarah, Isaac and Rebekah, Jacob and Leah, Rachel, Bilhah, and Zilpah. The nation traces its origins to God's call of Abram (Genesis 12:1-3). That call involved a series of covenant promises which were made to Abraham, then to his son Isaac, and then to Isaac's son Jacob. Genesis 12-50 records the spiritual journey of each of these three patriarchs and their families. The final story is that of Joseph, the son of Jacob. Joseph's story explains how the descendants of Abraham, Isaac, and Jacob came to live in Egypt.

This period can be viewed as the conception of the nation of Israel.

THE PERIOD OF EGYPTIAN SLAVERY AND DELIVERANCE:
Exodus, Leviticus, Numbers, Deuteronomy

Exodus 1 picks up where the Joseph story in Genesis left off: the descendants of Abraham, Isaac, and Jacob as residents of Egypt. Exodus 1 & 2 describe how the descendants of Abraham came to be slaves in Egypt.

This section of material involves four separate pivotal experiences:

- the Exodus experience – the story of God's deliverance of the descendants of Abraham, Isaac, and Jacob from their bondage in Egypt (Exodus 3-12). This story relates a conflict between the LORD (Yahweh), the God of the Israelites, and the many gods of Egyptian pantheon.
- the flight out of Egypt and wilderness journey (Exodus 13:17 – 18:27). This section relates various challenges the people faced as God led them *by the roundabout way of the wilderness* (Exodus 13:18).
- the encounter with the LORD at Mt. Sinai (Exodus 19 – 40). Three significant, life-shaping events took place during this year-long stay at Mt. Sinai:
  (1) the people entered covenant with God,
  (2) God gave the Law, and
  (3) the people built a tabernacle, precisely according to the instructions of God, so that God could dwell in their midst.

This section includes law materials. The Decalogue (Ten Commandments) and the Book of the Covenant relate to life in the covenant community while the laws in the book of Leviticus relate to the sacrifices and the priests who served in the tabernacle. Some of this material dates to a later period of time than the covenant at Sinai.

- the journey from Mt. Sinai and the wilderness wanderings (Numbers). Eighteen months after the Exodus out of Egypt, the people of Israel stood on the border of the Canaan, the Land of Promise. The book of Numbers relates the story of the people's rebellion against God and refusal to take the land. As a consequence, the people lived in the wilderness for another thirty-eight and a half years – for forty years total.

The setting of the book of Deuteronomy is the plains of Moab, on the edge of Canaan. A different generation is poised to take the land that God had promised to Abraham and his descendants. The book contains a series of addresses by Moses as he led the people in a renewal of the covenant. The title of the book means *second law*. It contains a second version of the Decalogue (Ten Commandments) along with an explanation of the covenant. Throughout the various discourses run a promise and warning: if you obey my statues and commands, then it shall go well with you. If you forget the LORD your God, then it will not go well with you. This *if ... then* promise and warning become the theological basis of the history known as Deuteronomistic history (Joshua, Judges, 1 & 2 Samuel, 1 & 2 Kings).

This period can be viewed as the birth of the nation of Israel.

THE PERIOD OF THE CONQUEST AND SETTLEMENT OF CANAAN:
Joshua, Judges

This section of Hebrew scripture describes the twelve tribes of Israel as they conquered the land of Canaan and settled it. The book of Joshua details the conquest, ending with a renewal of the covenant. The book of Judges describes life in the land. It describes a repeated cycle of unfaithfulness, oppression by enemies, repentance, and God's provision of a deliverer (judge) leading to blessing and peace.

This period can be viewed as the adolescence of the nation of Israel.

THE PERIOD OF THE HEBREW MONARCHY:
Historical books: *1 & 2 Samuel, 1 & 2 Kings, 1 & 2 Chronicles*
Prophets: *Isaiah 1-39, Jeremiah, Hosea, Amos, Micah, Nahum, Habakkuk, Zephaniah*

This section of scripture relates three movements in Israel's history:

- the transition to a monarchy under the guidance of Samuel, the prophet and judge.
- the United Kingdom under Saul, David, and Solomon
- the Divided Kingdoms of Judah & Israel.

In the Divided Kingdom, the northern kingdom was called Israel. It was made up of ten and one-half of the original twelve tribes. The capital of Israel was the city of Samaria. The nation was served by nineteen kings from nine different ruling families. Consequently, the nation's history was one of instability and political chaos. Israel fell to Assyria in 721 B.C.E. Assyria scattered many of the inhabitants of Israel throughout their vast empire, importing other conquered peoples to inhabit the land. These transplanted peoples intermarried with the people of Israel that Assyria had left in the land. In the New Testament era, these mixed-race people were called Samaritans. Their region was called Samaria after the original capital city.

The southern kingdom was called Judah. Judah's inhabitants came from one and one-half tribes: Judah and Dan. The nation took the name of the dominant tribe, Judah. Judah was served by nineteen kings. Each was a descendant of David, based on God's promise to David that one of his descendants would serve as king (2 Samuel 7:12-16). Judah survived the Assyrian crisis that led to the fall of the northern kingdom Israel. The prophet Isaiah served during that time of crisis. 150 years after the Assyrian crisis, Judah fell to Babylon in 586 B.C.E. In a series of defeats, various members of the king's family and members of the royal court were taken into Exile in Babylon. Other inhabitants fled to other countries such as Egypt. Ultimately, only the poorest of the land were left to inhabit the land. The prophet Jeremiah served during the Babylonian crisis.

This period can be viewed as the adulthood and death of the nation of Israel.

THE PERIOD OF THE BABYLONIAN EXILE AND RESTORATION
> Historical books: *Ezra, Nehemiah*
> Prophets: *Isaiah 40-65, Lamentations, Ezekiel, Obadiah, Haggai, Zechariah, Malachi*
> Wisdom literature: *Job*, selected *Psalms, Proverbs, Ecclesiastes, Song of Solomon*

This period of history encompasses the seventy year exile experience in Babylon and the return from exile made possible by the Persian king Cyrus. The exile experience was a time of great theological crisis for the nation. Everything upon which the nation's identity had been based was taken away: the kingship, the land, and the Temple. The people struggled with the question "why did this happen?" Their questioning led to differing theological positions, several of which reflected new ways of thinking:

- the exile experience was God's judgment on the nation (Lamentations, Deuteronomistic history)
- the LORD alone was God, the creator of heaven and earth and the Lord of history (Isaiah 40-55);
- suffering was redemptive rather than punishment for sin (Isaiah 53).

The people also struggled to find a new basis for identity in a foreign land. Their effort to establish a new identity led to the recording of their history and collection of their writings, leading ultimately to the writing and collecting of the Hebrew Scriptures. This effort to establish a new identity also led to an emphasis upon circumcision, keeping the Sabbath, and meeting together in small gatherings called the synagogue.

The reestablishment of the nation after the Exile is detailed in the books of Ezra and Nehemiah.

This period can be viewed as the resurrection or rebirth of the nation of Israel.

THE PERIOD BETWEEN THE TESTAMENTS:

Prophets: *Daniel*
Apocrypha/Deuterocanonical writings: *Tobit, Judith, Wisdom of Solomon, Ecclesiasticus* (Ben Sirach), *Baruch, The Letter of Jeremiah, Prayer of Azariah and the Song of the Three* Jews, *Bel and the Dragon, 1, 2, 3, & 4 Maccabees, 1 & 2 Esdras, Prayer of Manasseh,* additions to the books of *Esther* and *Daniel.*

After the destruction of Jerusalem in 586 B.C.E, the people of Judah lived as subjects to four different foreign powers: Babylon, Persia, Greece, and Rome. Babylon carried the leading citizens into Exile in Babylon between 597 and 586 B.C.E., where they lived in Exile. Others fled to Egypt in the face of the conquest. Many of the poorest continued to live in the land.

The Persian king Cyrus, after conquering Babylon, granted the Hebrew people permission to return to their home land and rebuild their Temple. Little is known of the life of the Hebrew people in the Persian Empire. During this period, many Jewish people continued to live outside the original homeland.

Alexander the Great conquered the Persian Empire, bringing the land of Judah under Greek control and influence. After the death of Alexander, the Greek Empire was divided among his warring generals. The land of Judah first came under the control of Ptolemy, but was later transferred to the control of the Seleucid dynasty. Under the rule of the Ptolemy dynasty in the fourth and third centuries B.C.E., the land of Judea enjoyed relative stability. Hellenism was embraced by the aristocracy of Judea and the Greek language became the universal language. In the second century B.C.E., the Seleucid kings replaced the Ptolemy's. This new line of kings sought to enforce the Hellenistic culture upon all within their domain, including Judea. Antiochus IV Epiphanes pressed the issue by invading Jerusalem in 169 B.C.E. He outlawed the Jewish religion, making it a crime to teach the Torah, offer sacrifices, observe the Sabbath, or circumcise their sons. He took control of the rebuilt Temple, making it a temple to Greek gods and offering swine on the altar as a sacrifice. Many of the Apocrypha/Deuterocanonical writings reflect this period. These writings emphasized Jews who were faithful in observing Jewish religious practices and traditions in the midst of foreign people.

The actions of Antiochus IV Epiphanes led to a revolt by the Hebrew people, led by the Hasmonean family. The revolt, which lasted twenty years, ultimately led to Jewish independence. This eighty year period of independence was filled with chaos as the various Jewish factions vied for control. It came to an end when the Romans took charge of the land in 63 B.C.E. The Apocrypha/Deuterocanonical works of 1, 2, 3, 4 Maccabees narrate this period.

This period continues the story of the Israel's rebirth and development.

PERIOD OF THE NEW TESTAMENT
   The life and ministry of Jesus: *Matthew, Mark, Luke, John*
   The birth and spread of the New Testament Church – *Acts*, letters to churches and individuals

The New Testament period is chronicled in the twenty-seven books of the New Testament – the Christian scriptures. The first four books present the gospel of the life and ministry, death and resurrection of Jesus the

Messiah. Each was written for a different audience in a different context. Yet, each proclaimed the same good news: Jesus of Nazareth was the Messiah who fulfilled the mission of the nation of Israel.

Mark is considered by most biblical scholars to be the first gospel written, sometime after 60 C.E. Mark's story outline was consequently used by the writers of Matthew and Luke. Thus, these three books are known as the Synoptic Gospels – the gospels that see with the same eye.

Mark's gospel emphasizes the actions of Jesus. It traces the spiritual journey of the disciples through three stages: blindness, seeing but not clearly, seeing clearly. See Mark 8:22-26 where the writer used the story of the staged-healing of the blind man as the outline of his gospel. In the first half of the gospel, the disciples do not recognize Jesus as the Messiah. They are blind. Following the healing of the blind man, they confess Jesus as the Messiah. They see, but not clearly. The last half of the gospel focuses upon Jesus' journey to Jerusalem and his last week in Jerusalem. During this time, the disciples "see" that Jesus is the Messiah, but struggle to understand that Jesus came as the Suffering Servant, not as a conquering messianic king. Jesus' death and resurrection were the second touch that led them to see clearly.

Matthew's gospel closely follows Mark's story line, but it emphasizes the teachings of Jesus. Written for a Jewish audience, the gospel is divided into five sections, paralleling the five books of Moses. Each section records what Jesus did, followed by a collection of Jesus' teachings. The sections are identified by the author's use of the phrase *when Jesus had finished* … (Matthew 7:29; 11:1; 13:53; 19:1; 26:1). Matthew presents Jesus as the fulfillment of the Law of Moses, the one greater than

Moses, and the Messiah. This gospel was written after the fall of Jerusalem in 70 C.E.

Luke's gospel appears to be written for a non-Jewish audience. It presents Jesus as the Messiah who proclaimed the Kingdom of God. The gospel's teachings reflect the nature of the Kingdom. Much of the material in Luke is not found in any other gospel. This material is recorded primarily in the section of Jesus' final journey to Jerusalem (see Luke 9:51). Like the gospel of Matthew, this gospel was written after the fall of Jerusalem in 70 C.E.

The gospel of John was the last gospel to be written, probably during the last decade of the first century. It was written to Jewish Christians who were being persecuted by the Pharisaic Jews who controlled the synagogue after the fall of Jerusalem. These Jewish Christians were being pressured to abandon the teachings of Jesus and re-embrace the teachings of Moses as disciples of Moses and the Law. The gospel portrays Jesus as the fulfillment of Jewish religious life: Sabbath, the great festivals, the Temple, and the Passover. Consequently, most of Jesus' ministry as recorded in this gospel took place in Jerusalem. The book is divided into four sections: the Prologue (1:1-18), the Book of Signs (chapters 1-12), the Book of Comfort (chapters 13-17), and the Glorification of Jesus in his crucifixion and resurrection (chapters 18-21).

The book of Acts was written as a companion to the Gospel according to Luke. (Compare Luke 1:1-4 and Acts 1:1-5.) Acts records the birth and growth of the early Church, beginning in Jerusalem and spreading throughout the Roman Empire. The first eleven chapters (1:1-11:18) describe the life of the early Jewish Church in Jerusalem. Beginning with 11:19, the writer focuses upon the ministry of the Apostle Paul, detailing his ministry of proclaiming the gospel to the Gentiles throughout the Roman Empire.

The other New Testament books are letters written to various churches and individuals. These letters reflect the struggles of the diverse congregations and contain instructions for living as the followers of Jesus in those settings.

This period can be viewed as the fulfillment of the nation of Israel in Jesus, the Messiah, and the continuation of God's mission through the followers of Jesus (the Church, composed both of Jews and Gentiles).

Learning to read and understand the Bible involves knowing the historical period and cultural context for which a particular book or passage was written. Understanding this overview of biblical history guides the reader in identifying such historical and cultural settings.

FOR PERSONAL REFLECTION:

1. This chapter presented eight different historical periods in the life of the Hebrew people. Each historical period reflects a different stage of spiritual understanding and development. In your spiritual journey, with which historical period do you identify? Why?
2. What in this chapter was helpful to you? Why? What in this chapter stirred discomfort or angst in you? What in this chapter did you not understand?

CHAPTER FIVE

HOW DO I KNOW WHAT TO BELIEVE?

We must no longer be children,
tossed to and fro and blown about by every wind of doctrine,
by people's trickery, by their craftiness in deceitful
scheming - Ephesians 4:14.

Few people read the Bible out of idle curiosity. Most read out of a desire to understand what the Bible says and means. Most read with the objective of understanding the Bible and what it teaches. In particular, most read with a desire to know the God that is revealed in the Bible.

The materials in the first four chapters are designed to address the readers' desire and objectives. They are intended to help the reader identify the divine truth(s) the Bible teaches – that is, what to believe about God and the ways of God. And the materials are intended to lay a foundation for putting those divine truths into practice – that is, how to live in relationship with God, living the ways of God.

A bonus feature of these materials is the foundation they provide for exercising spiritual discernment. Spiritual discernment is the Spirit-guided ability to recognize what is of God and what is not of God. It can be exercised in relation to what one hears in preaching or teaching, to what one reads, to what another says about God or God's will, to motivations, to behavior and practices, and to decisions that are being made.[1]

THE IMPORTANCE OF SPIRITUAL DISCERNMENT

The ability to exercise Spirit-directed discernment is a vital, yet frequently overlooked, skill. Apart from the practice of discernment, one is left without a means of knowing what to believe. Apart from discernment, one is in a vulnerable position. The writer of the book of Ephesians spoke of such vulnerability: *we must no longer be children, tossed to and fro and blown about by every wind of doctrine, by people's trickery, by their craftiness in deceitful scheming* (Ephesians 4:14). Without discernment, one is like a ship on the sea with no anchor to hold it fast in its position. Such a ship is at the will of the winds and the waves which carry it wherever they want. The one who does not know how to practice discernment is susceptible to the persuasiveness and manipulation of anyone who claims to know more.

Another danger associated with the lack of discernment is rigidity. Rigidity is the opposite of the vulnerability described in Ephesians 4. Rigidity represents an unteachable posture. The one who is rigid in his beliefs uses those beliefs as the standard to determine what is true, rejecting anything that is not in line with what is already believed. Such rigid beliefs are generally based upon one's heritage or culture rather than on a thoughtful, systematic study of scripture. Rigidly held beliefs seldom align with the revealed character of God or with the spirit and teachings of Jesus. This lack of alignment is because the reader searches the Bible for confirmation of what he already believes. He picks and chooses select texts, focusing upon those texts that validate his beliefs and ignoring those that challenge it. Thus, those who live out of a rigid, unmovable posture simply use the Bible to support, validate, and defend what they already believe.

The ultimate objective of reading and understanding scripture is to allow the truths taught in scripture to shape what one believes, how one thinks, and how one lives. Being shaped by the teachings of scripture requires a teachable spirit, one that is willing to learn and grow, adapt and change. It also requires the hard work of interpretation coupled with Spirit-guided discernment in knowing what to believe. Like the ability to interpret scripture, the ability to practice spiritual discernment is a skill that can be learned and developed.

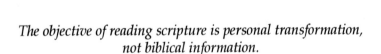

The objective of reading scripture is personal transformation, not biblical information.

INTERPRETATION, SPIRITUAL DISCERNMENT AND SPIRITUAL GROWTH

The writer of Ephesians associated the lack of spiritual discernment (knowing what to believe) with being spiritually immature. *We must no longer be children*

(Ephesians 4:14). Spiritual growth which leads to spiritual maturity inevitably involves discovering and embracing divine truth that leads to a change in how one thinks and, thereby, how one lives.

Acts 10 & 11 records such a growth experience in the life of the Apostle Peter. The account records five stages in the growth process.

❖ The confrontation stage, 10:9-16: Through a dream, God challenged what Peter already believed about non-Jews. Peter viewed Gentiles as unclean and, thereby, unacceptable. God challenged his thinking: *what God has made clean, you must not call profane* (verse 16). Note that the experience was possible because Peter placed himself in a position for God to speak. He went up on the roof to pray (10:9).

❖ The exploration stage, 10:17-33: Peter did not automatically embrace the new thinking. Rather, he explored this new way of thinking by responding to an invitation to go to the house of Cornelius, a Roman officer. He took other Jewish Christians along with him as he tested his thinking.

❖ The confirmation stage, 10:34-46: The new way of thinking about Gentiles was confirmed as Cornelius related his experience with an angel and as the Holy Spirit was poured out on those gathered to hear Peter preach. His experience led Peter to the conclusion: *I truly understand that God shows no partiality* (verse 34).

❖ The implementation stage, 10:47-48: Peter embraced the new thinking and began to act upon it by baptizing Cornelius and his household.

❖ The advocacy stage, 11:1-18: Peter not only incorporated this new way of thinking about Gentiles into his own life. He also taught this new way of thinking to others, advocating for a change in how other Jewish Christians thought about and related to Gentiles.

Note the role that divine truth played in this growth experience. The process of growth that resulted in change began with divine truth challenging what Peter thought and how he acted.

The Apostle Paul understood the role of spiritual truth in the transformation of one's life. In his letter to the Romans, Paul wrote: *do not be conformed to this world* (literally: stop being conformed to the world's old way of thinking), *but be transformed **by the renewing of your minds** so that you may discern what is the will of God,* (12:2 - emphasis added). Discovering and embracing divine truth transforms how one thinks and lives. It also empowers one to discern *what is the will of God.*

GUIDELINES FOR PRACTICING DISCERNMENT

The materials presented in Chapters 1-4 guide the reader in interpreting scripture. They also provide guidelines for exercising spiritual discernment.

❖ Does what I am hearing and considering reflect eternal, divine truth that is applicable to any time and any culture OR does it reflect the human wrapper of a particular historical, cultural period? Has divine truth been unwrapped from its human context?

❖ Is what I am hearing and considering in line with the merciful and gracious character of God revealed to Moses?

❖ Is what I am hearing and considering in line with the self-giving, servant love of God reflected in the life of Jesus?

❖ Is what I am hearing and considering reflected in the life, teaching, ministry, and spirit of Jesus?

❖ Is what I am hearing and considering an expression of grace OR a dimension of *if...then* thinking associated with the conditional merit-reward, earning-deserving approach to life?

❖ Does what I am hearing and considering focus upon the internal transformation of the heart, leading to spiritual maturity, OR is it a dimension of religious expectations focusing upon proper belief, proper behavior, and proper ritual?

❖ Is what I am hearing and considering an expression of the Kingdom of God OR is it a dimension of cultural, religious expectations?

FOR PERSONAL REFLECTION:

1. This chapter introduced the concept of spiritual discernment. Identify an experience of spiritual discernment from your spiritual journey.

2. How has your spiritual experience paralleled Peter's experience of spiritual growth?

   Identify an experience in which the way you thought was changed and, thereby, the way you related to others changed.

   What is your normal reaction to something that challenges what you believe?

3. The chapter presents guidelines to use in practicing spiritual discernment. What other guideline would you add?

   Practice using the guidelines.

4. What in this chapter was helpful to you? Why? What in this chapter stirred discomfort or angst in you? What in this chapter did you not understand?

EPILOGUE

The hard work associated with interpreting scripture and exercising spiritual discernment pays great dividends. Such efforts place one in a position for the Spirit to reveal what the Bible teaches. Knowing what the Bible teaches leads to knowing the character of God and the self-giving, servant ways of the Kingdom God. It guides one in living in relationship with God, trusting God's grace and goodness and forgiveness. It leads to a transformed life, being shaped in the likeness of Jesus. It leads to participation in God's quality of life – a life of depth, meaning, purpose, and joy that the writer of John's gospel called eternal life and abundant life. It leads to partnership with God in God's eternal purpose of creating a God-shaped world. It leads to participation in a spiritual community, committed to living the ways of God.

The one who would embark on a journey of studying the Bible does not walk alone. The Spirit of God summons him to the journey and walks alongside him. The Spirit guides every student of scripture, teaching spiritual truths. The Spirit calls him, like Peter, to embrace and put into practice such truths. The Spirit empowers him to live the truth that has been revealed. As a result, the student of scripture grows spiritually, being transformed by the Spirit through the renewing of his mind.

In addition, good biblical study is best done within the context of trusted spiritual friends. Such a context provides a safe arena to test one's thinking and explore the Spirit's guidance. The differing perspectives and experiences of such friends affirm, confront, refine, and expand one's understanding. The one who studies scripture alone robs themselves of this valuable refining resource. The solitary student is left within the narrow confines of his own thinking and experience.

This simple book is offered as a tool to use in the work of reading and interpreting scripture. It was written with the prayer that everyone who reads the Bible may understand the spiritual truths it contains, experience God's grace and, thereby, be transformed by the Spirit's renewing of their mind.

FOR PERSONAL REFLECTION:

1. What is your greatest "take away" from the study?
2. How is the way you read the Bible different because of this study?
3. How are you different because of this study?
4. What is your next step?

STUDY GUIDE
FOR GROUP DISCUSSION

The questions in this section provide a guide for discussion and dialogue in a small group setting. These questions are designed to engage the participants in processing the content of each chapter and their experience of it. They are based on, but not necessarily identical to, the Personal Reflection questions found at the end of each chapter. These questions are a tool for the group leader to use as a facilitator of conversation and sharing.

CHAPTER 1: Why is the Bible so Hard to Understand?

1. When did you first begin to read and study the Bible?

   How has your reading and study of the Bible changed over the years?

2. This book and this chapter in particular assume that many readers find the Bible difficult to understand.

   What kind of struggles have you experienced in reading and trying to understand the Bible? Relate a specific example of your struggle.

What emotion(s) does the struggle to understand stir within you?

Relate an example of something in the Bible that you do not understand.

2. This chapter describes the Bible as sixty-six ancient books that were written from a Near Eastern, prescientific, theological world view.

   What implications does this description raise for reading the Bible?

   How does this description change how you read and interpret the Bible?

3. This chapter indicated that reading out of scientifically trained thinking can be a barrier to understanding the Bible.

   How is that so? Give a specific example.

   How can such thinking be an advantage in reading the Bible?

4. This chapter indicated that another barrier to understanding what the Bible says and means is the already held beliefs that are the lens through which one reads the Bible.

   How can such belief-bias be a barrier?

   How does one deal with such a barrier?

Relate an example of a belief you surrendered through reading the Bible.

5. What in this chapter was helpful to you? Why?

    What in this chapter stirred discomfort or angst in you?

    What in this chapter did you not understand?

CHAPTER 2: How Do I Read the Bible so That It Makes Sense?

1. This chapter deals with the issue of interpretation. What is your reaction to the following statement from the chapter: *Every person who reads the Bible is also involved in interpreting it?*

2. This chapter offered a definition of the task of interpretation: *Interpretation is the task of discerning what the author was trying to say to his original audience.*

    Why is it important to understand what the original author was saying to the original audience?

    How does what the author was saying to the original audience relate to us today?

3. The chapter identified two different dimensions of scripture: the human dimension and the divine dimension.

    How are these two dimensions of scripture related?

What is the implication of these two dimensions of scripture for the task of interpretation?

What example did you identify of the human dimension of scripture?

What example did you identify of how the human wrapper can be confused with the divine truth?

4. What was your experience of using the interpretation model on a favorite passage of scripture?

5. What in this chapter was helpful to you? Why?

   What in this chapter stirred discomfort or angst in you?

   What in this chapter did you not understand?

CHAPTER 3: Isn't There a Simple Way to Understand the Bible? Guiding Principles and Foundational Truths

Because of the length of this chapter, small groups may want to take two (or more) sessions to deal with the following questions.

1. One of the guiding principles offered in this chapter was *follow Jesus' pattern of using scripture.*

   What is your perception of how Jesus used scripture?

   What guidelines can you identify from how Jesus used scripture?

2. This chapter asserted that the Bible does not present a single theological perspective.

   What is your reaction to this statement?

   Give an example of differing theological perspectives in scripture.

   What is the implication of this reality for interpreting scripture?

3. The first foundational truth that was presented was the character of God.

   What is meant by the character of God?

   What is your understanding of the character of God?

   In the description of the character of God presented in this chapter, what grabbed your attention or spoke to you?

   What is your understanding of God's judgement and wrath? How does judgement figure into God's character?

   What role does the character of God play in interpreting scripture?

4. This chapter addressed the eternal, divine purpose of God as revealed in scripture.

What was your reaction to the statement: *The eternal purpose of God revealed in scripture is larger than helping people escape hell and get to heaven?*

What did you understand the eternal, divine purpose of God to be as presented in this chapter?

What was your reaction to that description?

God's strategy *for achieving this divine purpose was to create God-shaped people - a family of sons and daughters who possess the Divine Nature and reflect the Divine likeness. By living the ways of God, this family is God's partner in God's eternal enterprise of creating a God-shaped world.* How does this description of God's strategy compare to your understanding of what it means to be a Christian?

This chapter used the terms *man-centered Christianity* and *God-centered Christianity.* What do these two terms mean? How are they different?

5. The Kingdom of God was a third foundational truth identified in the chapter.

   What is your understanding of the Kingdom of God?

   What place has the Kingdom of God had in your spiritual journey?

   How does the Kingdom of God relate to God's eternal, divine purpose?

What is the relationship between the Kingdom of God and the Church?

Review the 5 characteristics of the Kingdom of God presented in the chapter. Which one stands out to you? Which seems to be most difficult to live?

Identify an expression of the Kingdom of God in your church life.

6. The fourth foundational truth identified in this chapter was God's grace-based way of relating. How would you describe *grace* in practical terms?

   How does grace-based thinking and relating differ from *if ... then* thinking associated with merit-reward, earning-deserving approaches to life and relationships?

   Relate an example from your life of each kind of relating: grace-based, merit-reward.

   Relate when and how you first began to understand God's grace.

   What kind of struggle does grace create for you?

   How is religious life based on God's grace different from religious life based on *if ... then* thinking associated with merit-reward, earning-deserving approaches to God and one another? Relate an example.

7. What in this chapter was helpful to you? Why?

What in this chapter stirred discomfort or angst in you?

What in this chapter did you not understand?

CHAPTER 4: How Do All the Pieces Fit Together?

1. This chapter presented eight different historical periods in the life of the Hebrew people.

    Which period was most familiar to you? Why?

    Which period was most unfamiliar to you? Why?

2. With which historical period do you identify in your spiritual journey?

3. What in this chapter was helpful to you? Why?

    What in this chapter stirred discomfort or angst in you?

    What in this chapter did you not understand?

CHAPTER 5: How Do I Know What to Believe?

1. This chapter introduced the concept of spiritual discernment.

    What do you understand spiritual discernment to be?

    Why is spiritual discernment important?

What happens in the absence of spiritual discernment?

Relate an experience of spiritual discernment from your spiritual journey.

2. Peter's experience of spiritual growth – rooted in a new way of thinking – was presented in the chapter.

What part of the spiritual growth process spoke to you?

Relate an experience of spiritual growth in which the way you thought was changed and, thereby, the way you related to others changed.

What is your normal reaction to something that challenges what you believe?

3. The chapter presents guidelines to use in practicing spiritual discernment.

Which guideline is most important to you? Why?

What other guideline would you add?

4. What in this chapter was helpful to you? Why?

What in this chapter stirred discomfort or angst in you?

What in this chapter did you not understand?

EPILOGUE

1. What is your greatest "take away" from the study?

2. How is the way you read the Bible different because of this study?

3. How are you different because of this study?

4. What about our group experience was helpful to you? What would you suggest as a way of improving the group experience?

5. What is your next step? Where do you go from here?

CHAPTER NOTES:

INTRODUCTION

1. See the Ethiopian's question in Acts 8:31, *how can I (understand), unless someone guides me?*

CHAPTER 1: WHY IS THE BIBLE SO HARD TO UNDERSTAND?

1. Genesis 12 through 50 relates a fairly continuous story line, relating the experiences of Abraham and his descendants. The book of Exodus picks up the story line of Abraham's descendants after an extended period of time, as they lived as slaves in Egypt. The flow of the story in Exodus is interrupted at several points by the insertion of requirements for religious festivals (Exodus 12:14-20; Exodus 13:1-16), legal materials (the Book of the Covenant, Exodus 20:22-23:19), instructions for building a dwelling place for God among the people (the Tabernacle - Exodus 25:1-27:21; 30:1-38), instructions for priests to serve in the Tabernacle (Exodus 28:1-29:37), instructions for sacrifices in the Tabernacle (Exodus 29:38-46), and the description of building the Tabernacle

(Exodus 36:8-39:43). The story line is seemingly lost in the book of Leviticus, a book of religious regulations related to worship in the Tabernacle. It resurfaces in spots in the book of Numbers (Numbers 10:11-14:45; 16:1-18:32; 20:1-27:23; 31:1-36:13), ending with the people on the plains of Moab, prepared to enter the Land of Promise.

The books of Deuteronomy through 2 Kings are a unit known as Deuteronomistic history. These books tell the story of ...

- the people's conquest and settlement of the land of Canaan (Joshua and Judges),
- the establishment of a unified nation under a single king (1 & 2 Samuel, 1 Kings 1-11),
- the division of the nation (1 Kings 12ff),
- the destruction of the two nations (the northern kingdom of Israel by Assyria in 722 B.C.E; the southern kingdom of Judah by Babylon in 586 B.C.E.), resulting in the deportation of the Hebrew people into Babylon.

This history is written from the perspective of the book of Deuteronomy as an explanation of why the nation was destroyed and its inhabitants carried into Babylonia exile. Deuteronomy contains a series of speeches attributed to Moses in which he recounted the people's journey out of Egypt through the wilderness in anticipation of a covenant renewal celebration. That covenant renewal stressed an *if ... then* proposition. If the people obeyed the commandments of the Lord, it would go well with them in the land. If they forgot the LORD and disobeyed the commandments, they would lose the land. (See Deuteronomy 30:15-20.) This *if ... then* viewpoint is based on the belief that the ways of God produce a strong, healthy nation for all whereas abandonment of the ways of God undermine the strength and health of the nation. The Deuteronomistic history interprets Israel's history from that *if ... then* viewpoint.

The books of 1 & 2 Chronicles are a second historical narrative. This "history" is written from the perspective of Jerusalem and the southern kingdom of Judah. It begins with extensive genealogies, dating from Adam (Genesis 2 & 3) and running through the Babylonian exile. This history recounts the story of David and his lineage as kings of Judah. The history ends with a note regarding the Babylonian captivity (2 Chronicles 36:15-21) and the decree of the Persian King Cyrus allowing the exiles in Babylon to return to Jerusalem to rebuild the Temple (2 Chronicles 36:22-23).

The books of Ezra and Nehemiah relate the story of the return from Exile and the rebuilding of the Temple in Jerusalem.

2. Apocalyptic literature is a class of literature that was popular between 250 B.C.E. and 200 C.E. Although there are examples of this kind of writing in different Near Eastern cultures, it was particularly popular in the Hebrew nation. We have many examples of apocalyptic writings from the Hebrew people:

- in Hebrew Scripture (the Old Testament): portions of Daniel and Ezekiel, a small section of Isaiah, Joel;
- in the apocrypha: The book of Enoch, The Assumption of Moses, The Secrets of Enoch, The Book of Baruch, The Book of 4 Ezra;
- in the Christian scripture (the New Testament): Revelation, Matthew 25, Mark 13.

Apocalyptic literature developed out of and was written during times of great difficulty and trouble – generally times of suffering and great persecution in which the outlook seemed hopeless. Such hopeless situations often produce doubt, compromise, and abandonment of the faith (apostasy). Apocalyptic writing was developed to bring reassurance, stirring hope in the face of hopelessness, faith in the face of despair, faithfulness when the temptation to quit is strongest. Thus, the *purpose* of apocalyptic literature was to communicate assurance and comfort that fostered faithful endurance.

3. See the notice before Psalm 1, 42, 73, 90, 107.
4. See the opening verses of the prophetic works, such as Isaiah, Jeremiah, and Amos. Also see the opening verses of the writings of the Apostle Paul (Romans, 1 & 2 Corinthians, Galatians, Philippians, 1 & 2 Thessalonians, Philemon).
5. Deuteronomistic history refers to the books of Joshua, Judges, 1 & 2 Samuel, 1 & 2 Kings.
6. See particularly the book of Amos.
7. See Amos 2:6-8; 4:1; 5:10-15; 6:4-7; 8:4-6.
8. A definite shift in the view and treatment of women is reflected in Hebrew scripture. Before

the Exile, women held every position that a man did other than that of a priest or king. Deborah, for example, is identified as both a prophetess and a judge (Judges 4:4-5). After the exile, women were generally viewed negatively and often treated as property. Sirach, a book in the Apocrypha written after the Exile, reflects this negative view of women. Sirach 25:25 attributed the origin of sin to women: *from a woman sin had its beginning, and because of her we all die.* Also see Sirach 7:22-26 where children, daughters and wives are grouped with cattle; 9:1-9, warnings about women; 19:2, women, like wine, lead men astray; 22:3-5 & 26:10-12, negative view of daughters; 25:13-26 and 26:1-9, 13-18, negative view of wives. The negative view of women is reflected in the belief, during New Testament times, that it would be better for the Torah (Law) to be burned than taught to a woman.

A notable exception to this patriarchal viewpoint is found during the New Testament era in the Roman province of Macedonia. The Apostle Paul is often read as teaching this negative view of women. Paul actually taught the Kingdom principle that moves beyond social norms and embraces all as beloved children of God. In Galatians 3:28, Paul specifically applied this principle to women: *there is no longer Jew or Greek, there is no longer slave or free, there is no longer male and female; for all of you are one in Christ Jesus.*

An often overlooked fact is the women who are listed as pastors and leaders in the New Testament churches: Priscilla, Acts 18: 18, 24-26;

the four daughters of Philip who had the gift of prophecy (preaching), Acts 21:7-9; Phoebe, a deacon, Romans 16:1; Euodia and Syntyche, Philippians 4:2-3.

9. See Isaiah 1:17; Psalm 146:5-9.
10. See Exodus 8:8, 19, 25; 9:20, 27; 10:7-8, 16-17; 11:3; 12:33.
11. See Joshua 6:17-19; 1 Samuel 15:17-33.
12. See Isaiah 40:12-14, 21-31; 45:18-19; 48:12-13.
13. See Isaiah 41:25-29; 43:1-7; 43:11-21; 44:6-8, 24-28; 45:1-8; 46:8-11.
14. See Isaiah 42:24-26; 47:5-7.
15. See 40:18-20, 25-26; 41:21-24; 44:9-20; 46:5-7.

CHAPTER TWO: HOW DO I READ THE BIBLE SO THAT IT MAKES SENSE

1. A literal reading of the Bible is frequently presented as an act of faith. While such a perspective is indeed an act of faith, it is a misplaced and misinformed faith. To view the Bible as beyond error (inerrant, infallible) is to misplace one's faith. The true object of faith is God, not the Bible. The key question of faith is about God, not about the reliability of biblical facts: is God who Jesus revealed God to be as recorded in scripture? To view the Bible as beyond error also reflects a misinformed faith. It denies the human dimension of scripture while emphasizing only the divine dimension (addressed later in this chapter.) It refuses to do the hard work of thinking and discerning that is an inherent dimension of interpretation.
2. See Exodus 33:20 where God would not allow Moses to see God's face, i.e., a full view and

understanding of God. Moses was only allowed to see God's back, i.e., enough of God to satisfy Moses' desire without overwhelming Moses' free will.

3. Also see John 1:18, Colossians 1:15, 19; Colossians 2:9.
4. Compare Exodus 19:1-6 and 34:8-10a.
5. This model was first published in the author's Doctor of Ministry Project Report: *Equipping Believers with a Hermeneutical and Theological Foundation for Exercising Spiritual Discernment.*
6. Study Bibles vary in their usefulness. Every Study Bible reflects a theological slant. The discerning reader understands that reality and reads the notes in the Study Bible out of that understanding. Those Study Bibles that are most helpful introduce each book by providing historical and background information regarding the book. The notes provide historical and cultural information that help the reader interpret rather than telling the reader what a passage means.

CHAPTER THREE: ISN'T THERE A SIMPLE WAY TO UNDERSTAND THE BIBLE? GUIDING PRINCIPLES AND FOUNDATIONAL TRUTHS

1. Deuteronomistic history.
2. The revelation of the Divine Character is Exodus 34:6-7 is not the final scene in the Exodus covenant story. The story continues with Moses' response to this revelation, Exodus 34:8-9. Moses responded with adoration and worship, vs. 8, and then with self-abandonment to God and God's work, vs. 9. The culmination of the story is what God did. In the face of the broken, conditional

covenant, God restored the covenant with one that was unconditional. This restored covenant was based solely on who God is, not on who the people were – on what God did, not what the people did or did not do, vs. 10. The New Covenant proclaimed by the prophet Jeremiah (Jeremiah 31:31-34) picked up on the unconditional nature of the reestablished covenant of Exodus 34. The New Covenant was grounded in forgiveness, not obedience (Jeremiah 31:34).

3. Compare Psalm 103:6-14 and Jonah 4:1-2.
4. This phrase helps the reader understand the concept of God's judgement. Judgement is *not* an angry reaction from God to sinful behavior. Rather, judgement is an expression of a moral principle that is designed into the fabric of creation: actions have consequences. Rejection of the ways of God leads to chaos and destruction.

    The judgements proclaimed by the Hebrew prophets against the nations of Judah and Israel were the inevitable and unavoidable consequences of rejecting the ways of God and following the ways of the cultures around them. To seek national security through the ways of war made the nation vulnerable to the consequences of war: destruction at the hands of one's enemies. See Psalm 146:3-7 and Hosea 8:1-10; 11:3-7. When the affluent amassed wealth for their own luxury and comfort, while exploiting the poor and ignoring the plight of the poor, they not only rejected the ways of God, they also undermined the moral foundations of their society. See Isaiah 1:2-17, 21-23; 3:13-4:1; 5:1-13, 18-30; 10:1-4 and Amos 4:1-5.

Luke's gospel records the story of Jesus weeping over the fate of Jerusalem, the consequences of their rejection of the ways that make for peace (Luke 19:41-44). Jesus' grief over the impending fate of Jerusalem suggests that judgment grieves God.

In Romans 1:18-32, the Apostle Paul wrote to the house churches of Rome about *the wrath of God*. He spoke of God's wrath in terms of consequences, in line with the statement in Exodus 34:7c. Three times in the passage, Paul used the statement *God gave them over* (Romans 1:24, 26, 28). Each of the three statements described a condition that was worse than the previous one. God gave the people over to the consequences of their continuing choices.

The judgement of God and the wrath of God speak of how, apart from the intervening work of God, one receives the natural consequences of one's own choices. The Wisdom Literature in the Hebrew Scriptures reflects this foundational understanding. Deuteronomistic history interpreted the Exile experience from this perspective.

5. In Hosea 11:8-9, the prophet declared that God's compassion for God's people was greater than God's fierce anger. A compassion that was greater than wrath was a defining character trait of the Holy One of Israel (verse 9). Thus, God would respond out of compassion to restore the nation from the consequences of their self-destructive ways (Hosea 11:10-11).
6. See also Galatians 4:4-7; 5:16-26; Philippians 1:6; 8-11; 2:5-11.

7. This perspective interprets *the rulers and authorities in the heavenly places* as a reference to angelic beings in the heavenly realms. This interpretation is in line with Jesus' statement recorded in Luke 10:18 – *I watched Satan fall from heaven like a flash of lightning*. The understanding of Satan being cast from heaven is reflected in Revelation 12:1-4a. Another way of understanding this phrase is as a reference to civil and governmental authorities. In this interpretation, the Church as a community that bridges cultural differences (Ephesians 2:11-22) would be an expression of a different way of living in relationship, helping the rulers of the world to recognize the inherent flaw in a domination (power-over) way of living in community.

CHAPTER FOUR: HOW DO ALL THE PIECES FIT TOGETHER?

1. I was first introduced to this sweep of biblical history through the teaching ministry of Dr. Bill Tolar, although it is not unique to him. The outline presented in this chapter is an adaptation of Dr. Tolar's outline.

CHAPTER FIVE: HOW DO I KNOW WHAT TO BELIEVE?

1. See Acts 18:24-26; Ephesians 4:14-16; 1 Timothy 4:1-5; 2 Timothy 2:14-18, 3:1-9, 4:3-4; Titus 1:10-16, 3:8-11; Hebrews 5:11-14; 2 Peter 2:1-3, 3:17-18; 1 John 2:26, 4:1-6.

ABOUT THE AUTHOR

S teve Langford, also known as Pastor Steve, has given his adult life to the study and teaching of scripture in the local church. Within the religious communities in which he has walked and in the churches he has served, he is known as a gifted teacher. He is a lifelong student, having earned degrees in biblical studies from Howard Payne University in Brownwood, Texas, and of Southwestern Baptist Theological Seminary in Fort Worth, Texas, (M. Div., D. Min.).

Dr. Langford and his wife of 45 years have three sons - Josh, Jon and wife Linda, and Justin – and four grandchildren – Damon, Lillian, Scarlett, and Axel.

He currently serves as Senior Pastor at the First United Methodist Church of Georgetown, Texas.

CPSIA information can be obtained
at www.ICGtesting.com
Printed in the USA
FSOW02n1018120116
15597FS